EVIDENCE INFORMED LEADERSHIP IN EDUCATION

Also available from Continuum

Theory and Practice of Education, David A. Turner

Modernizing Schools, Graham Butt and Helen M. Gunter

Education, Democracy and Discourse, Knud Jensen and Stephen Walker

Evidence Informed Leadership in Education

Alison Taysum

continuum

Continuum International Publishing Group

The Tower Building, 11 York Road, London SE1 7NX

80 Maiden Lane, Suite 704, New York NY 10038

www.continuumbooks.com

First published 2010
Paperback edition first published 2012

British Library Cataloguing-in-Publication Data
A catalogue record for this book is available from the British Library.

ISBN: 978-1-8470-6562-9 (hardcover)
       978-1-4411-8056-8 (paperback)

Library of Congress Cataloging-in-Publication Data
Taysum, Alison.
Evidence informed leadership in education / Alison Taysum.
  p. cm.
Includes bibliographical references and index.
ISBN 978-1-4411-8056-8 (pbk. : alk. paper) – ISBN 978-1-4411-3156-0
(ebook pdf : alk. paper) – ISBN 978-1-4411-2892-8 (ebook epub : alk. paper)
1. Educational leadership. 2. School management and organization.
3. Decision making. I. Title.

LB2805.T395 2011
371.2'011–dc23   2011036194

Typeset by Pindar NZ, Auckland, New Zealand
Printed and bound in Great Britain

Contents

For Jo Taysum, Roy Taysum, Katie Taysum, and Peter Taysum with grateful thanks to Professor Richard Pring, Professor Helen Gunter and Dr Rene Saran.

Foreword

The author quotes Gunter, 2007: 'The field of education leadership in England is seriously ill and could be terminal'. And one problem with many who are terminally ill is that they fail to recognize the seriousness of their illness – or indeed that they are ill at all. Readers of this book would no longer suffer from such an illusion. In a careful, highly readable and reflective account of how significant learning takes place, the author challenges many of the underlying assumptions of courses and training programmes which aim at producing 'effective' leaders for the public services – those of education, health, social work and so on.

Those assumptions so often depend on the duality between theory and practice and on the seductive belief that thinking about practice begins with theory which is then translated into precise targets which, in turn, are cascaded down to the behaviours – those of the teachers, the nurses, or the social workers. Leaders produce the targets and insist upon the most effective means for achieving those targets. Teachers or nurses or doctors or social workers deliver those targets.

This book – gently but most effectively – challenges those assumptions. Intelligent practice is not like that. Arguing for an Aristotelian understanding of practical engagement, the author insists that the professional person comes to a situation with a range of beliefs and experiences which are embodied in their practice; being more intelligent about that practice requires the development of the skills of, and dispositions for, critical reflection upon those beliefs and experiences. They should not be ignored; they remain potent influences, even if unacknowledged, in the everyday activities of the professionals.

The author, therefore, argues for a very different approach to professional development of leaders – one which insists upon the openness to criticism, the pursuit of self-knowledge, the constant reference to evidence in the tentative conclusions reached, the embodiment of ethical considerations in the deliberations pursued, the realisation that only in communities of shared values and interests can institutions and their members flourish.

If this is true generally, it is even more so as different public services come together in order to produce a more comprehensive and holistic approach to the recipients of those services, as is envisaged in No Child Left Behind in the USA or in Every Child Matters in England. The temptation is for the creation of efficient top-down management; but the need is for greater respect for the professionals and the kind of leadership which develops the necessary skills and dispositions to engage in reflective and critical thinking together, thereby coming to share common beliefs and values.

This book, however, is far more than a philosophical defence of a different mode of thinking about leadership. It is soundly rooted in practice itself and, true to its general message, in the author's own self-knowledge – personal narrative, also, is an essential part of improvement, whether personal or professional. And there is a wealth of examples through the case studies carefully brought together. The author shows, therefore, the ways in which evidence-based professional development can be enhanced by systematic research which, properly conducted, is open to evidence of different kinds, which reflects upon the values and assumptions underpinning the selection of evidence, and which welcomes rather than shuns the critical scrutiny of others. As the author argues, in this understanding of leadership, the *process* of undertaking research is more important than the *product*, namely, the research findings. Intelligent practice is more important than theory disconnected from practice.

This is a most important book which needs to be widely read if the prevailing illness in education leadership theory is not to be terminal.

Professor Richard Pring,
University of Oxford

Chapter 1

Evidence Informed Leadership

Introduction

This book is for readers who are interested in learning how to make informed judgements using evidence when leading in educational settings. This book engages with a framework that enables critical reflection about the consequences of the decisions made. This is done by thinking what is best for the individual and what is best for the community/society and finding equilibrium in the balance of interests. This balance focuses on getting to know the self, and understanding the role the self plays in relationship with the community or communities. This is particularly important in educational communities of cultural diversity, where living together with differences calls for living together with understanding and tolerance.

Use of evidence informed leadership will be important to many professional stakeholders in educational settings including educationalists, those that work in health, crime and justice, social welfare, policy makers, government departments and associated professional bodies. The book explores how evidence-based practice and the thinking tools of *critical analysis* and *reflection* are important for evidence informed leadership in education. This is because these thinking tools help those using them to see their lives from a different perspective. These new perspectives may reveal new career and life trajectories that were previously either not thought possible, or simply not thought about. Therefore it is hoped that this book may offer tools to help educational leaders bridge the gap between the academy and the communities of non-academics it serves to engage in evidence informed leadership.

I have identified early in this book how important it is to know the self, and to have a lifelong commitment to getting to know the self better. When engaging in evidence informed leadership, it is important for the leader to think about their position in the decision making process. This will help the leader monitor how their open-mindedness may be curbed because of their position, and the extent to which their position may influence the outcome justly or unjustly. It is equally important for the reader to understand my own position in this book, and for the reader to make judgements about the warrants for the conclusions presented. As an author I recognize that no matter how much I try to objectify what I write in this book, I do not have a neutral position. Rather, a range of prior experiences have shaped my own perception of issues of social justice in terms of inclusion and exclusion. These have included my own education as a student of schools, colleges and latterly Universities culminating in me working in industry as a production manager, teaching in primary schools, serving as a school governor, gaining my Doctor of Education (EdD) and being an academic within higher education. I have worked at the University of Wolverhampton where I taught undergraduate students including teaching assistants, International students and students from Her Majesty's Royal Services. At the University of Leicester I teach International and National educational leaders, including headteachers and school business managers who are doing postgraduate research (PGR). I currently lead the EdD course at the School of Education, University of Leicester as the Postgraduate Tutor for the EdD. The postgraduate research programmes include masters, doctorates, and trainee teachers engaging with the Primary Postgraduate Certificate in Education programme which, on successful completion, usually leads onto Qualified Teacher Status.

To unravel all these experiences and to identify that a particular experience from the past makes me act in a particular way today is very challenging. Yet engaging with evidence informed leadership, demands that kind of approach. It is important to ask the self-critical questions that facilitate reflection on the evidence so that decisions made may be evidence informed. Evidence informed leadership therefore exposes how leaders may be judging a particular event/ person(s) in their educational institutions based on what has happened in their own lives before, or on the evidence. Realizing that personal experiences may have been shaping decisions, rather than decisions being rooted in the evidence on the table may be an uncomfortable revelation. However, such a revelation is both important and vital if leaders are to work for social justice in their educational communities. By working for social justice I mean offering an education that provides real opportunities to students so that they can make informed choices about their future lives, and careers. Applying such an approach to their everyday lives helps leaders make decisions based on a tried and tested framework of being critical and reflective. This is not something that happens and then does not happen. In other words being critical and reflective should not be turned on and off like a tap. Rather, in this book I am going to argue that it is important to make being critical and reflective a part of the grammar of thinking, or a habit. In this way, it is possible to make informed decisions whenever possible that have been made after due consideration of the evidence.

I have argued that it is important to be critical and reflective so that alternative perspectives are considered and the thoughts are turned back on themselves. Moreover, such critical reflection needs to influence practice and this is being *reflexive*. For me, becoming a reflexive researcher has invoked intellectual, emotional and spiritual responses where the spiritual is defined as the relationship a person has with their own life. These experiences have transformed my identity. This has positively influenced my praxis in ways I could not have imagined. I draw on Thomson's (2004) translation of Aristotle's lectures to define praxis as three elements. First, what an agent feels, encompassing a plan or intention. Second, what an agent chooses, guided by a desire to pursue truth with right purpose, such as respecting others. Third, what an agent does to change the current state. As such, praxis ties in closely with the foundation upon which knowledge was provided in universities which Barnett (1999) states as a commitment to four core values. These include:

- Search for truth
- Respect for others
- Tolerance of opposing views
- Commitment to the generation of new knowledge.

These core values arguably underpin the purpose of ethical educational research. Pring (2000) suggests ethics is the philosophical enquiry into the basis of morals and moral judgements from which rules and principles emerge. Pring (2005) continues that exploring in the light of evidence and argument is what it is to be human, and that such endeavour has no ending and should be regarded as a moral practice.

This book will build upon Pring's insights to help explore the tools needed to strive to conduct ethical educational research. The chapters reveal how the ground is uneven, since what is deemed to be ethical in one context may be deemed to be unethical in another. I provide evidence of what this means, and explain why thinking about such issues makes a valuable contribution to the continuing professional development (CPD) of educational leaders. It is arguable that the process of doing postgraduate research is as important as the conclusions of the research that inform practice, leadership, and that are disseminated and have value or impact in the field (Levin, 2004; Oancea and Furlong, 2007; Pollard, 2008). I will argue that the dissemination of research is a very ethical part of the research process. Thus how research is thought about in its design, how research is done, and the conclusions of the research, are all significant for three reasons. First, it is important for the development of educational leaders and their ways of thinking and doing (or praxis) within educational settings. Second, the potential positive influence the research may have on the praxis of the communities the leaders serve. Third, the value of the research or the impact of the research in the field. Postgraduate research potentially sheds light on relationships between members of the community and the institution, and one of the key roles of leadership is arguably about negotiating relationships (Taysum, 2008). Gunter and Rayner (2007) expand this by arguing that educational leaders are all those involved in education including educational professionals, local and national politicians those that work in health, crime and justice, social welfare, and administrators, professional researchers and consultants, parents, children and governors.

This book is timely because the debate continues regarding the importance of educational research to the development of educational settings. Particularly in light of Gunter's (2006) statement: 'The field of educational leadership in England is seriously ill and it could be terminal' (p. 6). This statement goes beyond England as Biddle and Saha (2005) identify. They carried out a wide-ranging project that examined how 120 school principals from major types of schools in the United States and Australia used educational research knowledge. Their findings revealed that over the last thirty years politicians, journalists, the academy from the field of education and beyond, right-wing critics of state schools and members of the research community have discredited the value of educational research (Taysum, 2007). Yet they also discovered that research played a significant part in the school principals' thinking. If postgraduate educational research is threatened, then so too is a very important source of continuing professional development for educational professionals who have much to offer the field. Indeed, the fact that educational professionals are engaging with educational research affords them the chance to contribute to the knowledge in the field, and therefore to have a voice. Without such a voice, knowledge creation may be dominated by policy makers, quangos, and inspection regimes that are funded by the government. This reduces the professional to passively receiving and transmitting the latest move from Whitehall into the classroom. Rather, the educational professional might use their knowledge, skills, expertise and postgraduate research to make evidence informed decisions when constructing curriculums and developing pedagogy to meet the needs of the students and legislation. Luke (2006) states pedagogy is the art and science of teaching. Pring (2005) argues that educational research is important for evidence-based policy and practice but he warns that analysis of what counts, as evidence is required. This is because educational research can only generate new knowledge and understanding when an appropriate focus is given to the logical framework of what is to be researched and understood. Moreover, this needs to take place in a world where the only certainty is that nothing is certain. These debates position the production and use of educational research as important for western governments, and with globalization, for the world. There is a need to investigate what works and what good praxis looks like and feels like (Gunter and Rayner, 2007).

This book examines the kind of thinking tools needed for such educational research. Critically reflecting, or in other words, examining opposing views and turning thought back on itself, arguably helps educational leaders confront taken-for-granted assumptions (Schön, 1987). Through this approach, they are able to begin to realize how they have contributed to the structures that have shaped what they can and can not think and do. By introducing new frames of reference, and critically reflecting on this new knowledge they may gain new insights into how the structures shape their praxis and they may be able to make more informed decisions about how to respond to and interact with the structures that shape their identities, and the identities of others. Leaders sharing their new ways of knowing and doing with members of their communities, may present others with windows of opportunity to become critical and reflective individuals. Their praxis, when informed by evidence from educational research, may present different life trajectories to people that may not have seemed possible before. The need for this is examined as a theme throughout the book and engages with the role evidence-based praxis might play in making the English Every Child Matters education policy contained within the social justice agenda become reality. Every Child Matters is a policy framework designed to meet its aim for every child, irrespective of background, to be healthy, stay safe, enjoy and achieve, make a positive contribution and achieve economic well-being. This agenda ties in very closely with issues of social justice contained within educational policy frameworks in the United States such as No Child Left Behind.

The chapters in this book explore the role evidence informed leadership in educational settings might play in actualizing the Every Child Matters, and the No Child Left Behind agendas. Here social justice is defined in terms of economic justice, cultural justice and the chances citizens have to associate with these and contribute to the making of these (Cribb and Gewirtz, 2003). By this it is meant that individuals may contribute to the policies that are put into practice that shape what they can and can not do. This book argues that evidence informed leadership has the potential to facilitate individuals' choices about how they contribute to the making of the policies, and about the kinds of career and life choices they may have within their communities. Moreover, it may help leaders facilitate citizens to make informed decisions about their contribution to society, in terms of earning a living and taking up civic responsibility.

The second chapter of the book provides the English Every Child Matters policy and the United States No Child Left Behind policy contexts as a backdrop to understanding the role of evidence informed leadership. In the past three decades politicians, journalists, the academy from the field of education and beyond, right-wing critics of state schools and members of the research community have discredited the value of educational research. Yet empirical evidence has revealed that research plays a key role in informing decisions made by educational leaders (Taysum, 2007; Biddle and Saha, 2005). This finding of fact is affirmed by Pring (2005) who argues that educational research is important for evidence-based policy and practice, but warns that analysis of what counts, as evidence is required. This is because educational research can only generate new knowledge and understanding when an appropriate focus is given to the logical structure of that which is to be understood. Moreover, this needs to take place in a world of uncertainty.

These debates position the production and use of ethical educational research as a matter of importance for nation states' governments. It is therefore important to present a critical backdrop to these key policies before engaging with the thinking tools required for such research that examines what works and what good practice looks like and feels like. Cribb and Gewirtz (2003) framework of social justice is introduced and used to think through the economic, and cultural implications of policy implementation and how community members can associate with this.

The third chapter of the book defines the field, which is leadership in education. The field of educational leadership is complex with contested boundaries. This chapter argues that a way of defining leadership in education is to engage with what it feels like for all those involved. This means examining how educational leadership may facilitate the formulation of shared understandings, which is how identities are formed. This is particularly important when different agencies from disciplines such as education, health, crime and justice, and social welfare are required to work together with the agenda of Every Child Matters that seeks to remove barriers to social justice.

Discourses about social justice in terms of economic justice and cultural justice are explored. It is argued that ways of joining up thinking and enterprise for the betterment of communities in educational settings need to be found. The chapter begins to explore that thinking tools may be required to facilitate evidence informed leadership as a way forward towards bridging the gap between diverse groups found in educational settings.

The fourth chapter explores how evidence informed leadership might contribute to communities in educational settings moving towards understanding themselves, each other and their role regarding civic responsibility. A new grammar of thinking is introduced and the potentially false dichotomy between theory and practice is exposed. The notion of praxis is carefully explained and contextualized. An explanation of what is meant by epistemology (the knowledge of what is) and ontology (what is) in simple English is also developed. Different 'ways of knowing' or 'epistemological approaches' are examined and this is tied in closely with evidence informed leadership.

The fifth chapter examines how preparing and developing public sector leaders to use the thinking tool of critical analysis may be important. The reason for this is that individuals may begin to question their 'gut reactions' and find them wanting. Confronting assumptions and behaviours in this way may contribute to a process of leaders getting to know themselves. Such an approach to knowing and doing has the potential to reveal obstacles. This opens the way for citizens to dislodge themselves from deterministic life paths or trajectories. Concrete detail, provided by evidence from extensive research is offered that sheds light on ways in which the academy supports the development of critical analysis with professional educationalists or groups of professional educationalists, to support 'peer-assisted learning'. This may occur through organized postgraduate research or through In Service Education for Teachers (INSET).

This chapter goes on to explore how preparing leaders in educational settings to use the thinking tool of systematic reflection may be important. The reason for this is that reflection is a process that turns thought back on itself that enables a human being to think about what they are doing as they do it (Schön, 1987). This approach is very important because it allows practitioners to gain insight, which may enable framing and reframing of situations to occur, this enables dominant discourses to be challenged, bringing meaning to the messiness of day-to-day life.

The sixth chapter explores the tensions between who is actively associating with their educational communities, and who is marginalized. The role of dialogue is explored as a method for how communities might contribute to the interpretation of policies and structures that shape their lives. How communities might use dialogue to reach provisional consensus is explored. To do this, dialogue builds on discourses that examine issues surrounding positionality, dispositions and what it means to search for truth while reconciling issues of power among different cultures. Here the notion of evidence informed leadership in education is considered in terms of facilitating the building of trust and the need for such leadership to be ethical.

The seventh chapter brings the strands of the first six chapters together. The argument I make is that through research undertaken in communities of practice supported by the academy, educational leaders are presented with the opportunity to develop a systematic, critical and reflective approach to research, policy and curriculums. Their intellectual work underpins informed judgements about praxis in their local, particular and complex settings. Such reflexivity is evidence informed leadership. This chapter presents evidence from the field that reveals how educational leaders have used postgraduate research to work for social justice. Evidence is presented about how educational leaders' reflexive research has caused transformation of identity (Delamont and Atkinson, 2004). The evidence also shows how reflexive research enhances educational opportunities while meeting social justice agendas contained within policies such as Every Child Matters, No Child Left Behind, and 'Russian Education – 2020: A model of education for an economy based on knowledge' (2008 Moscow, [in Russian]).

The final chapter presents a summary where the argument that it is important to move forward with evidence informed leadership in educational settings is presented. This is particularly so, if the Every Child Matters, and the No Child Left Behind agendas are to be met. Evidence informed leadership is important because it enables educational leaders and the communities they serve, to critically analyse and reflect. This may lead to reflexive praxis leading to people having greater self-knowledge and knowledge of their environment. Such an approach may enable citizens to recognize new career and life trajectories that were not considered possible before. It may also enable citizens to think through how they might associate more with and contribute more to their own community. This might be achieved through developing their understanding and tolerance of others, and taking up shared civic responsibility working within policies that shape economic and cultural structures. Evidence informed leadership may be one way of moving towards removing barriers to social justice. Moreover, there is scope for the academy to support communities in developing evidence informed leadership through postgraduate research programmes. It is hoped that such endeavour will bridge the gap between the academy and communities in educational settings.

The book draws upon extensive research of those engaging with postgraduate research in England, the United States and Russia. The sample draws from postgraduate programmes in ten higher education institutions in these three geographical regions with some fifty respondents. Respondents that took part in the research were international researchers into postgraduate education, postgraduate programme providers, and educational leaders who are doing or who had recently completed postgraduate research. These leaders included superintendents, principals, headteachers, former headteachers who are now consultant heads, teachers on project (leaders who bridge the gap between the district level and the school administration level), and classroom teachers with leadership responsibilities. These leaders share their experiences of their postgraduate research learning journeys.

For the purpose of this research, the learning journeys start from the point of entry to the postgraduate research programme, to the stage in the programme the leaders have reached when they engaged with this research. However, throughout the research, respondents frequently locate their understanding of their learning journeys within their wider lived lives (Taysum, 2006). Therefore, the main thrust of this research examines the learning journeys of school leaders during their period of time doing postgraduate research, but recognizes respondents' claims that these journeys are located within meta-learning journeys of whole lived lives. The learning that takes place on these journeys encompasses all the construing and re-construing (Senge, 1997) the leaders may do in response to the world about them. Such learning may or may not underpin a shift in identity (Thomson, 2006).

The postgraduate research programmes engaged with in this research are masters programmes that may lead to Doctor of Philosophy (PhD) and Educational Doctorates (EdDs). Where respondents are engaging with doctorates they are located in one of four phases. Phase 1 is when they have just begun their doctoral studies. Phase 2 is when they are working on assignments or working towards a review of their work to progress from Advanced Postgraduate (APG) to full PhD student. Phase 3 is where the respondents are working on their thesis. Phase 4 is when a leader is now a doctor or in the process of doing revisions to their thesis post oral examination where a defence of the thesis is given called a viva voce. The intention of this sample is to yield valuable evidence regarding how the leaders describe and understand their learning at different points of their postgraduate learning journeys.

The research acknowledges that human beings' understanding of the world and their place within it is constructed (Cohen *et al.*, 2001). Donmoyer (1990) argues that educational professionals are interested in individuals and as such generalizations have less utility than qualitative research here presented. The respondents who have generously given their time to be interviewed and who have provided the empirical evidence for this study were chosen because leadership features in the postgraduate programmes they are involved in. It is worthy of note that the progamme providers and researchers are field leaders and have published internationally. They also have a plethora of experience in schools and HEIs (Taysum, 2006).

The position I take in this book is critical and my position is that narrative accounts of life stories are a way of recognizing and capturing others' social realities. It is important to represent these different perspectives however, I do not represent all the respondents in this book because there is not scope to do so. Rather I use excerpts to reveal arguments and positions from within the oral texts. The critical approach is intended to enable the reader to interpret and associate with the arguments in the book. The book does not aim to present generalized truths (Gunter and Taysum, 2008).

Pseudonyms have been chosen for this research so that anonymity and confidentiality can be maintained (AERA, 2000; BERA, 2004; ESRC, 2010). This research takes a comprehensive view of the perceptions of the programme providers, professional researchers, and educational leaders. Where appropriate the book draws upon documentary analysis, particularly with regard to the local and particular policy contexts the researched are located in. This is important because the book approaches and engages with how leaders use evidence informed leadership to operationalize the Every Child Matters policy in England and the No Child Left Behind policy in the United States implicit and explicit social justice agendas. Reference is also made to the Russian education policy 'Russian Education – 2020: A model of education for an economy based on knowledge' (2008).

References

American Educational Research Association (AERA) (2000), *Ethical Standards of the American Educational Research Association* [online]. Available at: http://www.aera.net/uploadedFiles/About_AERA/Ethical_Standards/EthicalStandards.pdf (accessed 24 May 2010).
Barnett, R. (1999), *Realizing the University in an Age of Supercomplexity*. Buckingham: Open University Press.

Biddle, B. and Saha, L. (2005), *The Untested Accusation*. Lanham, MD: Scarecrow Education.

British Educational Research Association (BERA) (2004), *Revised Ethical Guidelines* [online]. Available at: http://www.bera.ac.uk/publications/pdfs/ETHICA1.PDF (accessed 24 May 2010).

Cohen, L., Manion, L. and Morrison, K. (2001), *Research Methods in Education*. London: Croom Helm.

Cribb, A. and Gewirtz, S. (2003), Towards a sociology of just practices; an analysis of plural conceptions of justice. In C. Vincent (ed.), *Social Justice Education and Identity*. London: RoutledgeFalmer.

Delamont, S., and Atkinson, P. (2004), Qualitative research and the postmodern turn. In M. Hardy and A. Bryman (eds), *Handbook of Data Analysis*. London: Sage.

DfES (2003), *Every Child Matters*. London: HMSO.

Donmoyer, R. (1990) Generalisability and the single-case study. In E. Eisner and A. Peskin (eds), *Qualitative Inquiry in Education: The continuing debate*. New York, NY: Teachers College Press.

Economic and Social Research Council (ESRC) (2010), *Framework for Research Ethics* (FRE) [online]. Available at: http://www.esrc.ac.uk/ESRCInfoCentre/ImagesESRC_Re_Ethics_Frame_tcm6-11291.pdf (accessed 24 May 2010).

Gunter, H. M. and Rayner, S. (2007), Modernising the school workforce in England: challenging transformation and leadership? *Leadership*, 3 (1), 47–64.

Hardy, M. and Bryman A. (2004), *Handbook of Data Analysis*. London: Sage.

Kuz'minov, I. and Framin, I. (eds) (2008), *Russian Education – 2020: A model of education for an economy based on knowledge*, in Russian (RE). Moscow: Publishing house of HSE.

Levin, B. (2004). Making Research Matter More. *Education Policy Analysis Archives*, 12 (56), 1–22.

Luke, A. (2006), Teaching after the market from commodity to cosmopolitan. In L. Weis, G. McCarthy and G. Dimitriadis (eds), *Ideology, Curriculum and the New Sociology of Education Revisiting the Work of Michael Apple*. London: Routledge.

Oancea, A. and Furlong, J. (2007), Expressions of excellence and the assessment of applied and practice-based research. *Research Papers in Education*, 22 (2), 119–37.

Pollard, A. (ed.) (2008), *Quality and Capacity in UK Education Research*. Report of the first meeting of the UK's Strategic Forum for Research in Education, 16th and 17th October, Harrogate.

Pring, R. (2000), *Philosophy of Educational Research*. London: Continuum.

—— (2005), *Philosophy of Education*. London: Continuum.

Senge, P. (1997), *Fifth Discipline: Art and practice to self-training organization*. Moscow: Olympus Business.

Schön, D. A. (1987), *Educating the Reflective Practitioner*. London: Jossey-Bass.

Taysum, A. (2006), *A Survey of the Learning Journeys of School Leaders Doing the Doctorate of Education in England*. Birmingham: University of Birmingham.

—— (2007), EdD research: does it have a future in developing educational leaders? *New Zealand Journal of Educational Leadership*, 22 (2), 22–36.

—— (2008), School Leadership in G. McCulloch and D. Crook (eds), *The Routledge International Encyclopedia of Education*. London: RoutledgeFalmer.

—— (2008), The Role of Research in Developing Educational Leadership for the 21st Century. *American Educational Research Association Annual Conference*, New York.

Taysum, A. and Gunter, H. (2008), A critical approach to researching social justice and school leadership in England. *Education, Citizenship and Social Justice*, 3 (2), 183–99.

Thomson, J. (2004), *Aristotle The Nicomachean Ethics*. London: Penguin Books.

Thomson, P. (2006), Miners, diggers, ferals and showmen: school-community projects that affirm and unsettle identities and place. *British Journal of Sociology of Education*, 27 (1), 81–96.

U.S. Department of Education, Office of Elementary and Secondary Education (2002), *No Child Left Behind: A desktop reference*. Washington, DC.

Chapter 2

Policy and Evidence Informed Leadership: Every Child Matters and No Child Left Behind in Focus

This chapter provides the English Every Child Matters policy and the United States (US) No Child Left Behind policy contexts as a backdrop to understanding the role of evidence informed leadership. In the past three decades politicians, journalists, the academy from the field of education and beyond, rightwing critics of state schools and members of the research community have discredited the value of educational research. Yet empirical evidence has revealed that research plays a key role in informing decisions made by educational leaders. This finding of fact is affirmed by Pring (2005) who argues that educational research is important for evidence-based policy and practice, but warns that analysis of what counts as evidence is required. This is because educational research can only generate new knowledge and understanding when an appropriate focus is given to the logical structure of that which is to be understood. Moreover, this needs to take place in a world of uncertainty.

These debates position the production of knowledge that emerges from ethical educational research as a matter of importance to nation states' governments. It is therefore important to present a critical back drop to these key policies before engaging with the thinking tools required for such research and to examine what good practice looks like and feels like.

The context, and the problem

Arguably a goal for education is to prepare the next generation for civic work and civic responsibility; to contribute to constructing and sustaining the economic and social infrastructures of individual communities, individual countries, and collectively, the global village. Here a community or educational community is moving towards being defined by the way it is collectively understood by all those affected by it, regardless of local, national and international contexts within which it is bounded.

Key to education is the knowledge that is chosen to be imparted to learners, and the knowledge that the learners access, use and transform. This is problematic because different ideologies underpin different forms of knowledge, and therefore the education process is political and engages with issues of power. Rather than educational policies building on what works, and what does not, education has arguably been responding to political agendas of government policy makers (McDermott, 2007)

The issues of power are significant and over time different countries may or may not have experienced shifts in the balance of power in terms of dominant, and sub-dominant ideologies that underpin their policies. At the same time, tensions need to be handled with regard to different ideologies underpinning educational policy. Pressure may be exerted on one hand in the form of educational policy that aims to gain a country's infrastructure competitive advantage in the economic global arena. Particular training may prepare a work-force by transferring skills. On the other hand, the same educational policy may demonstrate support by recognizing absolute poverty, low income communities, and/or economic exploitation, and promote an ethic of care (Noddings, 1994). Educational policy may aim to develop high energy consuming, and polluting technologies, while at the same time promoting ecological and agronomical practices that will sustain life as we know it in the world we live in today. Educational policy is therefore highly complex, since policy as text is interpreted as policy as discourse in educational institutions using Stephen Ball's two-dimensional approach to policy as product and process (Ball, 2006). I begin to shed light on what might be going wrong in the realization of the noble aims of the Every Child Matters and the No Child Left Behind social justice agendas. This presents difficulties because a 'one size fits all' educational policy potentially needs to be adopted and adapted by an educational community. I begin to shed light on the problems that a one-size-fits-all national educational policy may face when being adopted and adapted by a particular educational institution in a particular local and particular place. Through meaningful and worthwhile dialogues with all those affected by educational policy, the language of educational policy may become understood. Those affected by the educational policy may wish to take a more active part in the co-construction of the educational policy. Such a democratic approach to the construction of educational policy needs to be explored. Internally motivated citizens may take an active role in such civic work, accepting responsibility and enjoying the rights of a just system. Externally motivated people might take a more passive role within the socio-economic infrastructure, responding to particular stimuli such as tests, and rewards, with an instant gratification, shoot from the hip, fight or flight approach. A third group may have a combination of internal motivation and external motivation. Here community members may be internally motivated and desire to take an active part in democratic civic life. They may also wish to seek the benefit of the wisdom of an elect council. In any of these scenarios, the values that underpin the different ideologies found in educational policies may benefit from being revealed to the educational community in an open and transparent way for due consideration. In this way community stakeholders, and in particular learners, may begin to make informed choices about whether they wish to be internally motivated, or externally motivated, and may begin to consider alternative life and career trajectories that may include civic responsibility, previously hidden from them. The heart of education policies is arguably the well-being of the learner and therefore it is fundamental that classrooms are not stressful places to be in (Traxson, 2001). Moreover, Troman (2008) argues that love and commitment to care need to be at the heart of domestic and work commitments. Arguably, an ethic of care and being part of a regime that induces stress are incompatible.

The aim of this chapter is to consider what policy is, and to explain the interplay between policy that is written and policy that is realized in context. How policy should be analysed is explored using Ball's (2006) framework. The English Every Child Matters policy agenda, and the United States No Child Left Behind policy agenda and their histories are analysed using this framework. This is because these are the agendas that educational leaders need to work within in England and the United States. However, these policy agendas also influence other nations. Two such nations are Russia with the 'Russian Education – 2020: A model of education for an economy based on knowledge' (2008, in Russian) (Pogosian, 2008), and Pakistan 'The National Education Policy 1998–2010' (Taysum and Iqbal, 2008; Taysum, Pogosian and Iqbal, 2009).

Policy as text and policy as discourse

Policy is an elusive concept that can prove extraordinarily difficult to define. Part of its complexity arises from the many different forms policy can take. Blakemore (2003) suggests that policies may be articulated as aims, goals or statements but that these focus on what ought to happen. Education policy is therefore frequently presented in government publications, party manifestos and politicians' speeches. This is 'grand policy'. Institutions, organizations and even individuals will also have policies as aims, goals and statements, but these may also be realized through actions that are not published and therefore not explicit, not necessarily understood, not open to public scrutiny or dialogue, and not open to a democratic process where a provisional consensus may be achieved.

Shields (2007) argues that the notion of democracy can be inadequate and provides a fictitious but real case study to support this claim. The case study reveals a school principal exploring options to better serve the community and raise standards in her school having failed to secure a much needed bond to finance school improvements. Evidence from a Florida school demonstrated that a change to a balanced school calendar raised grades from a 'D' to an 'A' on their high stakes test. Initial discussions with the case study school staff demonstrated that teachers at the school were enthusiastic to change the school calendar to help support 75 per cent of the school population who were disadvantaged. The change in calendar would create time and space to give additional support to facilitate learning. Meetings were arranged after much research and discussion. The media got involved which caused some misunderstanding, and a further meeting was scheduled where 25 per cent of the school parents attended. Most of these parents were 'white and middle class' and represented the most affluent and highest achieving school community members. These parents recognized that the change in school calendar would not positively influence their children's learning. Of the parent population 75 per cent did not attend the meeting to discuss the change of the school calendar. It was argued that these represented the disadvantaged school population. A reason given for their non-attendance was that they take several jobs to try to 'keep up'. The demands on their time prevented them from attending the meeting. Moreover, taking several jobs potentially prevented them from supporting their children's learning such as reading to them. However, this positioning is interpreted by The Superintendent and The Board as lack of interest in their children's education. This claim was evidenced by the 'democratic' vote against the change in school calendar. Yet the principal acknowledged that the proposed reform to the school calendar had failed without being given a chance. The notion of democracy appears inadequate in this case if democracy is defined as a minority deciding for the majority. The notion of democracy and its relationship with dominant discourses, knowledge and power needs to be interrogated, and the role of policy within this relationship needs to be explicit and citizens need to be able to associate with it (Cribb and Gewirtz, 2003; Taysum and Gunter, 2008).

Grace (1995) argues against a reductionist approach to the way policy is implemented in educational organizations where management solutions to problems are presented as prescribed ways for dealing with particular problems. This disregard for a person's ability to solve problems and make decisions that are informed by evidence in complex situations is troubling. Some things may be working very well within schools, thus making resistance to changes very important. However, the chance to resist is lost if the local and particular context is bleached out. Such detachment of grand policy from the communities it shapes limits the ways in which leaders can realize policy in their educational communities for social justice. Preventing leaders from doing their job stops them from serving their communities and therefore prevents leaders from providing best value. The importance of this can not be under rehearsed because communities' identities are shaped by their wider environment. The wider environment includes the economic and cultural conditions that are local, national and global. Fraser (1997) argues that social justice itself is being divided into redistributive justice for economically defined classes on the one hand, and a justice of recognition that connects with issues of identity for the individual and for communities. Educational policies can help to couple together the economic and the cultural, but this may not be necessary in areas where economic well-being and cultural recognition are enjoyed for example by the middle classes. The danger here is that the dominant voices of the middle classes may shape educational policy leaving educational leaders in areas of low socio-economic status to work creatively and courageously with policy to address social justice both economically and culturally. This is challenging if resources are limited and legislative and accountability requirements need to be met. Manna and Petrilli (2008) cite an associate superintendent from Buffalo, New York who states: 'we move on data. We're moving on scientifically based research. We're not going to rely on creativity to support these children. We're not looking for teachers to do their own thing' (p. 71).

One of the key issues here is that policy needs to be thought through by looking at it in different ways – or critically. This may be done collectively as a dialogue so that all those affected by the policy are able to associate with it (Cribb and Gewirtz, 2003). Bell and Stevenson (2006) argue that research into 'leadership' has replaced research into policy. This prevents the critique of dominant discourses and the science of how to deliver or realize educational policy. Moreover, the moral imperative is detached from the day to day busy-ness of learning and teaching (Hodgkinson, 1993), and the chance to recognize communities may be lost.

To be able to recognize minority and marginalized community groups it is important for those realizing policy to access and then possess the necessary codes, networks of classification, and shared meanings (Strain, 1998) of the minority and marginalized communities. New understandings may then be generated from the definition of 'democracy' which may be found wanting.

Redefining democracy is an important first step that enables the educational leader to work on behalf of those least advantaged in society and educational systems without pathologizing or essentializing them. The educational leader who engages with this kind of intellectual work may find accessing such codes uncomfortable because they may realize they have unwittingly been part of the misrecognition of minority and marginalized communities. On the other hand, the educational leader works within structures of high levels of public account-ability with high-stakes tests in the United States and England, and they may feel unable to take on a role that challenges educational policy. In this scenario the leaders collude with dominant discourses, but their position needs to be considered very carefully. It may be that challenging policy may cost them their jobs. This is clearly a devastating consequence for the leader personally, and any professional influence is lost. Therefore negotiating and choosing what is worth fighting for is an essential part of an educational leader's thinking

(Shields *et al.*, 2009). However, such choices have not always been so challenging. Examining a brief potted history of educational policies since the second world war in England and the United States reveals that there have been shifts in the balance of power between the education profession and the state with regard to practice.

Histories of educational policies in England and the United States – structures that shape identities

This section demonstrates that England and the US experienced two similar shifts in educational policy at similar times since 1944 to the present day. The English and US policy context is presented for each shift.

The Norwood Report 1943 underpinned the 1944 Education Act in the UK sometimes labelled 'The Butler Act' after the then Secretary of State for Education. This was a pivotal point for secondary education in the UK and the act laid down the foundations for secondary education with the introduction of secondary grammar schools, secondary technical schools, and secondary modern schools (Bartlett *et al.*, 2001). In the UK the Newsome Report in 1963 labelled 'Half our Future' had an aim to make an offer of more equitable provision to the 'average' and 'below average' student with an ideology that every child mattered and all potential was recognized and nurtured. The Circular 10/65 (DES, 1965) by the then Labour Education of State Antony Crosland was to eliminate 'separtisim' (Maclure, 1973). This shift towards comprehensive education was followed by the Plowden report (DES, 1967), which was child-centred, and Strain (1998) suggests: 'the learner's "busy-ness", [was] an indication then of fruitful learning in process' (p. 9).

In 1945, after the Second World War, The Federal Government of the United States launched a Life Adjustment Education Programme however segregated schools were constitutional (Spring, 2008). In 1954 the *Brown v. Board of Education*, decision of the United States Supreme Court ended 'separate but equal' schooling in The United States to conform with the Equal Protection Clause of the Fourteenth Amendment to the United States Constitution. This was followed by the 1958 National Defense Education Act where the Federal

Government enlisted schools in the Cold War against the Soviet Union. In the 1960s the United States wanted to educate the poor because poverty and cultural 'deficiencies' were framed as the causes of low academic attainment and in 1964 Head Start began as part of Federal War on Poverty (Spring, 2008). The Elementary and Secondary Act (ESEA) was authorized in 1965 with a focus on Title 1 with an aim to break the cycles of poverty and cultural deficiencies. The shift was to inculcate middle class culture through educational policy transmitted to the classroom. Stein (2004) cites Congressman Jacobs (D, IN) call for cultural training that would compensate for bad mothering. Stein (2004) also cites Senator Ralph Yarborough (D, TX) who argued that cultural deprivation should be attacked at source. Such aggressive language was directed towards poor mothers who were deemed not good enough to bring up their children. However, there is complexity here, because it is not clear if the Congressmen here cited had access to the voices of the working class mothers they refer to. Congressman Yarborough for example was one of the leaders of the progressive liberal wing of the Democratic Party and was the only member of Senate representing a former Confederate State to vote for every Civil Rights Legislation from 1957–1990 (Cox, 2010). Therefore these Congressmen may have been trying to improve the situation but may not have shared the symbols and language of the working class mothers they were trying to serve. Therefore the Congressmen and the working class mothers did not have a shared social reality. Such complexity is discussed in the next chapter. Congress did go on to reauthorize the Elementary and Secondary Education Act (ESEA) in 1966 and in 1967. The language was one arguably shaped by the Vietnam War as passionate narratives presented ESEA as a way to 'save' poor children and develop communities (Stein, 2004). It is important to note that the hall mark of this period in both England and the United States was a search for equality of provision and improvement of provision.

In the 1970s a further shift of educational policy was experienced in England and the United States. In England in 1976 the Black Papers were presented that attacked the Plowden report. Three themes appeared. First, academic standards were in decline. Second, dangerous politically motivated teachers were preaching revolution, socialism, egalitarianism, feminism, and sexual deviation. Third, the schools were full of indiscipline which predicated the construction of 'moral panic' (Ball, 2006). The moral panic emerged from the espoused decline in traditional values and a dualism was presented where democracy was pathologized, and tradition, discipline and authority was the common sense view at that time (Ball, 2006). The Black Papers facilitated the intellectual basis for affirming an anti-progressive ideology thus challenging child-centred education. Callaghan's speech at Ruskin College presented a need to focus on a more technocratic education with greater accountability (Bartlett and Burton, 2003). The international context linked to world trade and oil prices are bleached out of this discussion.

In the United States, the Title 1 reauthorization debates of the 1970s focused on presenting measurable outcomes that would provide performance indicators for government spending. Policy effectiveness could be evaluated through measurable results. The debate moved towards academic targets for the children rather than the cultural deficiencies of the children. The shift in part was the consequence of a misallocation of resources. Stein (2004) cites superintendants' misallocation of resources such as spending money on the interior design of their offices that was money intended for 'poor children'. On the strength of this the reauthorization of Title 1 focused on structures that would enable evaluation of local educational programmes rather than replacing them. At the time when measurable outcomes were put in place a new word; 'pre-delinquents' was introduced into the policy. The implications were that the policy beneficiaries, previously recognized as poor, were now constructed as 'potential criminals' (Stein, 2004).

In the 1980s the United States experienced stability with only two reauthorizations to the Elementary and Secondary Education Act. The first reauthorizing occurred in 1981 to consolidate and cut spending. The second reauthorization was in 1988 that shifted the focus away from children of poverty to schools the children of poverty attended.

England experienced further embedding of policies of accountability in 1988 with the Education Reform Act (DES, 1988), which presented a compulsory curriculum for all maintained schools in England and made religious education compulsory. Parents could choose which school to send their child, which was a move that introduced competition for school spaces. Thus the control of schools was centralized while appearing to devolve power with the Local Management of Schools (LMS). The 1992 Education Schools Act (DfE, 1992) established the Office for Standards in Education (Ofsted) as an independent body that inspected primary and secondary schools (Chitty, 2004). Ofsted brought about accountability and the language of attainment and efficiency was further endorsed (Strain, 1998).

A plethora of acts then followed, that continued to develop the agenda of the 1988 Education Reform Act. Whitty (2008) states the 1992 White Paper (DfE, 1992) moved more money away from the Local Authorities. The 1997 Education Act developed standards of attainment with targets (Whitty, 2008) and the language of effectiveness Sammons *et al.* (1995). The policies focusing on the Every Child Matters agenda then followed with the Every Child Matters Green Paper (2003), The Children's Act (2004) and The Education Act (2005). The latter provides legislation underpinning the transformation of Children's Services as set out in the Every Child Matters agenda. *Every Child Matters: The Framework for Inspection* (Ofsted, 2005) was published as a strategic document for Directors and Managers of Children's Services. The Further Education and Training Act (2007) followed that focused on the Further Education Sector, and on provision regarding the Learning and Skills Council for England. Diversity was key to the education and training to be made available to learners with a focus on industrial training levels, and joined-up thinking between industry, the third sector and Higher Education Institutions.

While these rapid and successive changes took place in England, the United States introduced the No Child Left Behind (2001) legislation. The focus of this education policy was improving the academic achievement of the disadvantaged; preparing, training and recruiting high quality teachers; language instruction for limited English proficient and immigrant students; promoting informed parental choice, and innovative programs; and flexibility and accountability. It is worthy of note that No Child Left Behind features the phrase 'Scientifically based research' more than one hundred times. However, Manna and Petrilli (2008) argue that this term is used inconsistently throughout the policy. I now consider what counts as 'research' and explore ways in which stronger relationships can be built between educational policy, educational research and dialogues with communities. I explore ways in which educational communities may be able to engage with civic work and democracy. I also consider the kinds of issues that are presenting barriers to the written policy being translated into practice for social justice within educational communities.

Policy as text; Every Child Matters and No Child Left Behind

The background to Every Child Matters was the tragic death of Victoria Climbie. The Every Child Matters agenda attempted to bring together agencies and disparate strands of educational and social policy so that such a tragedy would not be repeated. The aim was for the community to recognize children and young people and to provide services that met their needs. This was to be realized while raising standards of achievement, having an extended schools agenda, reforming the workforce, and presenting alternatives to failing schools such as academies (Gordon and Broadhead, 2007). Every Child Matters sets out five aims for children: be healthy; stay safe; enjoy and achieve; make a positive contribution; and achieve economic well-being. The Children's Trust provided a framework for change where all children's services worked in partnership to secure the outcomes of children linked to Every Child Matters with a goal of having a network of children centres and extended schools by 2010 (ibid.). It was recognized that the well-being of children and overcoming disadvantage could not be achieved if services worked in isolation without an overarching coherent strategy. The key was to be responsive so that prevention and early intervention could ensure children and families developed resilience (ibid.).

An independent evaluation of extended schools (September 2006) found individuals and families were able to access learning and influence life chances by improving relationships, raising aspirations, and improving attitudes and self-confidence. This Gordon and Broadhead (2007) argue was achieved through the core offer of:

High-quality wraparound care . . . available 8am–6pm all year round; a varied menu of activities, such as homework clubs and study support, sport, music tuition, dance and drama, arts and crafts, special interest clubs such as chess and first-aid courses; parenting support including information sessions for parents at key transition points and family learning sessions to allow children to learn with their parents; swift and easy referral to a wide range of specialist support services such as speech therapy, child and adolescent mental health services, family support services, intensive behavior support and sexual health services; wider community access to ICT, sport and arts facilities, including adult learning. (p. 6)

The United States is also working towards engaging community and parents through the No Child Left Behind agenda that empowers parents. United States Department of Education, Office of Elementary and Secondary Education, (2002) states Title 1 of No Child Left Behind:

Requires local school districts to offer public school choice to students in schools identified for improvement, corrective action, or restructuring so that no student is trapped in an underperforming school. School districts must provide transportation for eligible students, subject to the 20 per cent rule . . .;

requires school districts to permit low-income students attending chronically under-performing schools to obtain supplemental educational services from a public or private sector provider that has been approved by the state. Faith based organizations are eligible to apply for approval to provide supplemental education services;

requires school districts to spend an amount equal to 20 per cent of their Part A funds for transportation of students who exercise a choice option or for supplemental educational services, unless a less amount is needed to meet all requests. These funds do not have to be taken from Title 1 allocations, but may be provided from other allowable federal, state, local, or private sources;

notifies parents of school choice and supplemental educational services options; requires districts to 'promptly' notify parents of eligible students attending schools identified for improvement, corrective action, or restructuring of their option to transfer their child to a better public school or to obtain supplemental educational services;

establishes parents 'Right to Know' provision. Requires local school districts to annually notify parents of their right to request information on the professional qualifications of their children's teachers. (p. 15)

However, in both these policies as texts the parents and students appear to be passive, meaning that things happen to them in a one-way direction, with little space for talkback or for engagement in dialogue. Professor Helen Gunter and I have used Cribb and Gewirtz (2003) framework in a paper that takes a critical approach to researching social justice and school leadership in England (Taysum and Gunter, 2008) and I use this approach in this book. Cribb and Gewirtz (2003) present three concerns of justice – distributive, cultural and associational. Taysum and Gunter (2008) cite Fraser (1997) who suggests distributive justice engages with: exploitation, where the wages of human capital from manual workers are awarded to those who did not do the work; economic marginalization where poorly paid work may or may not be available or there is no work; deprivation where the material standard of living is not of minimum standards, and is often illegal (Bertaux and Bertaux-Wiame, 1981). There may appear to be a superficial equality of opportunity through distributive justice and the language of Every Child Matters and No Child Left Behind as above, however the equalizing of the distribution of resources is not addressed.

The second concern of Cribb and Gewirtz is cultural justice where cultural domination ensures a common sense that replicates the cultural domination for future generations. Cultural justice exists where there is recognition (Bourdieu, 2000) of cultures and where there is respect and tolerance for others (Cribb and Gewirtz, 2003). This appears to be where Every Child Matters and No Child Left Behind are at now; seeking to work for change so that all cultures living together respect one another and recognize one another. However, such a politics of recognition of many cultures requires individuals from those cultures to be part of a democratic process. The kind of democratic process needs to be defined in the ways that have been identified by Shields (2007) earlier in this chapter. By using democracy as a mask to ensure that the dominant groups get what they want through a 'democratic process' is not the kind of democracy that is required for citizens to engage meaningfully in worthwhile civic work. Therefore Cribb and Gewirtz's (2003) final strand of their social justice framework of 'association' is important.

The associational is about making public and transparent spaces for all people within the community to be part of the decision making process that shapes what they can and can not know and do. Arguably any enterprise that includes individuals having equal rights and responsibilities in the choices made that affect their lives is democratic and is the first important step towards well-being. This is important because Rowland (2008) cites a report from 14 February 2007 from the United Nations Children's Fund that positioned the United States and Great Britain as the worst two countries in the industrialized global village in which to be a child. UNICEF examined 40 factors including poverty, deprivation, happiness, relationships, and risky or bad behaviour. In a table of 21 economically developed nations, the United States and Great Britain came 20th and 21st respectively. For such findings to be revealed, it is clear the well-being of the child and, or learner is not at the heart of education. Wells (2008) argues that this reflects the *general lack of well-being for citizens in the community* and demonstrates how *the gap between the rich and poor continues to grow* and she cites the Opportunity Agenda (2007) the number of Americans living in poverty has risen over the last eight years. There is insufficient space to explore how the socio-economic infrastructure is reflected by inequalities in education here. The reader may explore this further in Taysum (2006). Rather two key themes, testing and issues of performativity, will be examined with regard to policy as discourse.

Policy as discourse: testing performance, performativity and the consequences for children and young people

There are arguably two kinds of assessment for learning, one is summative, and one is formative. Summative assessment provides a snapshot view of a candidate's performance in a particular test in a particular context. Formative assessment is assessment for learning (AfL) that provides an opportunity to promote students' learning. There is not scope in this book to engage with the practices of assessment for learning and the reader is recommended to look at Black, McCormick, James and Pedder (2006) to explore assessment for learning practices that encourage learning. The Standardized Assessment Tests (SATs) in England and the SATs in the United States are summative. It is worthy of note that the acronym for the United States SATs stood for Scholastic Assessment Tests but in 1996 this was dropped so the initials of SAT no longer mean anything (Atkinson and Geiser, 2009). The tests are summative and predict readiness for particular pathways forward for learners to Higher or Further Education in academic or vocational areas, or to work, or both. However, Atkinson and Geiser (2009) present an interesting view of the value of summative testing that is not part of the learners' subject grades that have emerged from continuous learning of a curriculum in class. Atkinson and Geiser have found that subject examination grades outperform the SATs as predictive indicators of success in college. It is not clear why this is the case and why grading standards have such variation across schools. They argue that using SATs may standardize assessment across all schools and states, but they state:

> Irrespective of the quality or type of school attended, cumulative grade-point average in academic subjects in high school has proven consistently the best overall predictor of student performance in college. This finding has been confirmed in hundreds of 'predictive-validity' studies conducted over the years, including studies conducted by the testing agencies themselves. (Atkinson and Geiser, 2009, p. 3; see Morgan, 1989, and Burton and Ramist, 2001, for useful summaries of studies conducted since 1976).

Yet it is clear that SATs are influencing Kindergarten through to Year 12 which is the equivalent of reception to Year 12 in England. Moreover, SATs are influencing minority and marginalized groups getting access to universities. Atkinson and Geiser (2009) argue that the University of California (UC) requires candidates to take the SAT 1 and achievement tests. Their rationale is that the SAT 1 test consistently failed to predict college performance as well as the subject achievement tests. UC focused on an outreach project to low-performing schools in California and built relationships with 300 of the lowest-performing schools in the state. Yet evidence revealed that the students from these 300 hundred schools were facing questions on the SAT 1 that they had not covered in class. Their consistently good achievement in their grades as a result of continual assessment was not recognized and this was interpreted as the students not being good enough to attend UC regardless of their record in high school. This had a dramatic affect on students' aspirations, motivation, and self-esteem and was interpreted that the students were not good enough to attend UC (Atkinson and

Geiser, 2009). This has clear implications for the learners' and what Finnigan and Gross (2007) refer to as well-being. Further McDermott (2007) rehearses:

> A graduation test will only encourage poor or less than able teachers and administrators to strengthen their holds on classrooms and schools because their success will be determined not by broad aspects of learning or happy faces or meeting needs, but by the testing results, regardless of how those results were obtained (New Jersey Assembly, 1978, p. 6A). (p. 90)

In The Universities Council for the Education of Teachers 'Towards a Position Paper' (Gordon and Broadhead, 2007) argue that the United Nations Convention on the Rights of the Child identify that play is a fundamental entitlement of the child, but that play at Key Stage 1 (in England 5 years old to 7 years old) 'is likely to be tokenistic as long as SATs exert their impact' (p. 15). An alternative argument against SATs is summed up by the American Educational Research Association (AERA) Position Paper on Pre Kindergarten through to Year 12 (Pre-K–12) Education (AERA, 2000) that argues that test scores alone should not determine the life chances of a learner. Rather, a minimum standard is offered that where a test score does not reveal a learner's proficiency then an alternative means should be provided. Atkinson and Geiser (2009) argue that:

> Curriculum-based achievement tests are the fairest and most effective assessments for college admissions and have important incentive or signalling effects for our K–12 schools as well: They help reinforce a rigorous academic curriculum and create better alignment of teaching, learning, and assessment all along the pathway from high school to college . . . A first order of business is to put admissions tests in proper perspective: High School grades are the best indicator of student readiness for college, and standardized tests are useful primarily as a supplement to the high-school record. (p. 2)

Moreover, Atkinson and Geiser (2009) cite Princeton economist Jesse Rothstein who makes the conservative estimate that studies of validity that do not consider the Socio Economic Status (SES) of students exaggerate the predictive ability of the SAT by 150 per cent. Further, Atkinson and Geiser present the Sackett *et al.* (2009) argument that the power of the SAT to predict college perform-ance is not reduced by SES. However, Atkinson and Geiser (2009) argue that the Sackett *et al.* (2009) study only looked at the relationship between the SAT and the students' first year grades (college outcomes), and did not examine the High School Grades Point Average (HSGPA) in isolation. The kinds of activities that HSGPA engage with reflect the kinds of activities that students will engage with in the first year of college. Therefore Atkinson and Geiser suggest it is arguably no surprise that the HSGPA are accurate predictors of first year college outcomes.

The key issues that emerge from the Every Child Matters and No Child Left Behind education policies that have implications for other nations are that the policies are built on a testing regime that identifies if students have attained a necessary level. As McDermott (2007) argues such testing identifies some students as successes and others as failures at a very early stage in their young lives. The consequential attack on a child's self-esteem is potentially affirmed at the SAT1 and subsequently throughout any approach to lifelong learning. Such a symbolic attack rather than a physical attack is damaging to a child and nega-tively affects a child's well being, which Bourdieu (2000) calls symbolic violence. It is therefore not surprising that the United States and Great Britain have come 20th and 21st respectively in the well-being of the child as published by UNICEF in their report of 14 February 2007. However, the affects on the professional identity of the teacher who is working within the testing regimes, needs to be examined. Troman (2008) studied primary school teachers in England and his findings revealed that the main problem was:

> how to maximize test scores, for these were the fundamental units of assess-ment of the school, and the teaching and learning which took place. For the institution's survival, this needed to be done while also maintaining the moti-vation and commitment of staff and pupils, and satisfying external inspectors that policies were being implemented in a cost-effective manner. (p. 622)

The approach to 'teaching to the test' and the prescribed national curriculums that teachers need to work within has contributed to a culture of 'performativity' (Ball, 2004). Ball argues that there is a relationship between performativity, the testing regimes, and the neoliberalist market forces. Schools need to be located at the top of the league tables, and therefore select their students when working within an environment that enables competition for school spaces. Ball (2004) argues those schools that can: 'select their students either formally or informally, are more able to control their league table position and their reputation generally' (p. 151). Ball goes onto argue that the students who are challenging to teach and may not perform well in General Certificate of Secondary Education (GCSE) examinations are the most expensive to teach and they may damage the reputation of the school. Such students are therefore excluded from school. Ball (2004) argues: 'we have seen a massive growth in the number of students excluded from school in the UK since 1991' (p. 151). Ball cites from his extensive research with headteachers that the best strategy for improving GCSE *performance* in the league tables is to manage the student intake. Tables of *performance* underpin a culture of *performativity* shaped by market forces. Within such environments, Johns (2009) argues that teachers are finding it challenging to meet the diverse needs of their students and are having to find creative and courageous ways of teaching their students which is extremely challenging. Such evidence indicates that it is important that teachers are given the space to think about their teaching and that they are able to engage their students in meaningful and worthwhile ways with the child, young person's and *learner's* well-being at the centre of the learning and teaching process. Educational leaders arguably need to negotiate policy and free up safe spaces for teachers to work collaboratively and democratically with the community to achieve this. Rodriguez (2009) argues for such collaboration to be truly effective educators need to hear the authentic voices of their local communities. This is examined in depth by Wells (2003) with regard to dialogic inquiry. Taysum (2009) argues that educational leaders may take up a role of 'public intellectual'. Such intellectual work engages with critiquing and reflecting upon the evidence from their postgraduate research and enables them to confront the 'common sense view'. If this does not occur the inequities identified earlier may become more deeply embedded in current and future generations through policy or case law. Such legislation is very often developed to remove barriers to social justice, but fails because it does not contain the necessary codes, networks of classification, symbolic activity and shared meanings (Strain, 1998) to recognize minority and marginalized communities.

As Cribb and Gewirtz (2003) state social justice needs to connect with a politics of distribution, a politics of cultural recognition, and a politics of association so that the communities can associate with and contribute democratically to the policies that shape what they can and can not do. Transparent dialogues between those making social justice policies and legislation, those implementing social justice policies and legislation and those whose identities are shaped by the social justice policies and legislation may help to realise the noble aims of the education policies No Child Left Behind and Every Child Matters. This theme is examined by Gordon (2003) when she argues that education restricts the working class, and provides the only opportunity to participate in a technological expression of the industrial structures from the nineteenth century.

Conclusions

To sum up, mapping the recent history of educational policies there has been a shift in the balance of power from control of what is taught in the classroom from the teaching profession to Government/Congress. This shift has happened due to the implementation of national curriculums and high stakes testing in England and through the implementation of high stakes testing regimes in the United States. This has happened with the right intentions. The right intentions are to give every child an equal opportunity with regard to the No Child Left Behind Title 1 reforms and Every Child Matters reforms. However, teachers are performing in the classroom by teaching to a test and/or prescribed curriculum that ignores a 'readiness to learn'. This is not authentic for the learner or the facilitator of learning and ultimately results in a misrecognition of marginalized and minoritized groups (Wells, 2008). Such misrecognition has arguably contributed to UNICEF placing the United States and Britain as 20th and 21st respectively in a table of 21 economically developed nations after examining 40 factors including poverty, deprivation, happiness, relationships, and risky or bad behaviour

The written policy needs to be considered as policy negotiated practice where the rubber meets the road. Such negotiation needs to be community centred and learner centred. Putting learners at the centre of the learning process is an important first step to making the learning meaningful and worthwhile. This important first step may enable learners to become motivated because they can associate with the curriculum and what they are learning. Further, associating with the learning and enabling the students to enjoy learning may protect them from a testing system that labels them as failures and prevents them from achieving their full potential. This has massive implications for the well-being of the learner, their families, and the community. The next step needs to be engaging communities 'democratically' so that they can associate with the learning process. Association of this kind may build relationships within communities based on evidence, positive regard, and respect for people who become citizens fully engaged in civic work.

The book now explores how this might be achieved in a step-by-step process and focuses on possible solutions to the problems this chapter raises. It does this by presenting tools to facilitate evidence informed leadership that help confront 'common sense views' when working for social justice and moving from policy as text to policy as discourse in communities.

References

AERA (2000), *American Educational Research Association Position Statement on High-Stakes Testing in Pre K–12 Education*. From American Education Research Association: http://www.aera.net/policyandprograms/?id=378 (accessed 20 April 2009).

Atkinson, R. C. and Geiser, S. (2009), Reflections on a century of college admissions tests. *American Educational Research Association Annual Conference* (pp. 1–21). San Diego: Center for Studies of Higher Education, University of California Berkeley Campus.

Ball, S. J. (2004), *The Routledge Falmer Reader in Sociology of Education*. London: Routledge.

Ball, S. J. (2006), *Education Policy and Social Class*. London: Routledge.

Bartlett, S., Burton, D. and Peim, N. (2001), *Introduction to Education Studies*. London: Paul Chapman Publishing.

Bartlett, S. and Burton, D. (2003), *Education Studies Essential Issues*. London: Sage.

Bell, L. and Stevenson, H. (2006), *Education Policy: Process, themes and impact*. London: RoutledgeFalmer.

Bertaux, D. and Bertaux-Wiame, I. (1981), Life stories in the bakers' trade. In D. Bertaux, *Biography and Society*. Beverly Hills, CA: Sage.

Black, P., McCormick, R., James, M. and Pedder, D. (2006), Learning how to learn and assessment for learning: a theoretical inquiry. *Research Papers in Education*, 21 (2), 119–32.

Blakemore, K. (2003), *Social Policy: An introduction*. Buckingham: Open University Press.

Brown v. Board of Education (1954), 347 U.S. 483. Available at: http://caselaw.lp.findlaw.com/scripts/getcase.pl?court=US&vol=347&invol=483 (accessed May 2010).

Bourdieu, P. (2000), *Pascalian Meditations*. Cambridge: Polity.

Burton, N. and Ramist, L. (2001), *Predicting Success in College: SAT studies of classes graduating since 1980. College Board Research Report no. 2001–2.* New York: College Board.

Chitty, C. (2004), *Education Policy in Britain.* New York: Palgrave Macmillan.

Cox, P. L. (2010), Ralph Yarborough Biography. Available from http://www.biographybase.com/biography/Yarborough_Ralph.html (accessed 23 March 2010).

Cribb, A. and Gewirtz, S. (2003), Towards a sociology of just practices: an analysis of plural conceptions of justice. In C. Vincent (ed.), *Social Justice Education and Identity.* London: RoutledgeFalmer.

Central Advisory Council for Education (ACE) (1963), *Half our Future* (The Newsom Report). London: HMSO (accessed July 2008).

Department for Education (1992), *Choice and Diversity: A new framework for schools.* London: HMSO (accessed July 2008).

Department for Education and Science (1997), *Education Act 1997.* Available at: http://www.opsi.gov.uk/acts/acts1997/ukpga_19970044_en_1 (accessed July 2008).

Department of Education and Science (DES) (1965), *The Organisation of Secondary Education.* Circular 10/65. London: HMSO.

—— (1967), *Children and their Primary Schools* (The Plowden Report). London: HMSO (accessed July 2008).

—— (1988), *The Education Reform Act 1988.* London: HMSO (accessed July 2008).

—— (2004), *Children Act 2004.* (Every Child Matters). Available at: http://www.opsi.gov.uk/acts/acts2004/ukpga_20040031_en_1.htm (accessed July 2008).

Department for Education and Skills (2005), *Education Act 2005.* Available at: http://www.opsi.gov.uk/acts/acts2005/ukpga_20050018_en_1 (accessed July 2008).

Department for Children, Schools and Families (2007), *Further Education and Training Act 2007.* http://www.opsi.gov.uk/acts/acts2007/ukpga_20070025_en_1 (accessed July 2008).

Department for Education and Skills (2003), *Every Child Matters.* London: HMSO.

Elementary and Secondary Education Act (1965), US Statutes at Large, Public Law 89–10. Available at: http://www.eric.ed.gov:80/ERICDocs/data/ericdocs2sql/content_storage_01/0000019b/80/33/d3/2d.pdf (accessed May 2010).

Finnigan, K. and Gross, B. (2007), Do accountability policy sanctions influence teacher motivation? Lessons from Chicago's low-perfoming schools. *American Educational Research Journal,* 44 (3), 594–629.

Fraser, N. (1997), *Justice Interruptus: Critical reflections on the 'postsocialist' condition.* New York and London: Routledge.

Gordon, J. (2003), A shoelace left untied: Teachers negotiate class and ethnicity. *Urban Review,* 35 (3), 191–215.

Gordon, K. and Broadhead, P. (2007, April), *Every Child Matters and Teacher Education: A Universities Council for the Education of Teachers Position Paper.* London: Universities Council for the Education of Teachers.

Government of Pakistan (1998), *National Education Policy (1998–2010).* Islamabad: Ministry of Education.

Grace, G. (1995), *School Leadership Beyond Education Management: An essay in policy scholarship.* London: The Falmer Press.

Gunter, H. (2005), Conceptualizing research in educational leadership. *Educational Management Administration and Leadership,* 33 (2), 165–80.

Hodgkinson, C. (1993), *Educational leadership: the moral art.* Albany, NY: State University of New York Press.

Johns, J. R. (2009), Abriendo caminos: peer coaching of culturally relevant pedagogy for teachers of adolescent emergent bilinguals. *American Educational Research Association Annual Conference.* San Diego, April 2009.

Kuz'minov, I. and Framin, I. (eds) (2008), *Russian Education – 2020: A model of education for an economy based on knowledge* in Russian (RE). Moscow: Publishing house of HSE.

Maclure, J. (1973), *Educational Documents England and Wales 1816 to the Present Day*. London: Methuen.

Manna, P. and Petrilli, M. J. (2008), Double standard? 'Scientifically based research' and the No Child Left Behind Act. In F. Hess, *When Research Matters. How scholarship influences education policy* (pp. 63–88). Cambridge, MA: Harvard University Press.

McDermott, K. (2007), 'Expanding the moral community' or 'blaming the victim'? The politics of state education accountability policy. *American Educational Research Journal*, 44 (1), 77–111.

Morgan, R. C. (1989), *Analysis of the Predictive Validity of the SAT and High School Grades from 1976–1983. College Board Report*. New York: College Board.

National Defense Act (1958), US Statutes at Large, Public Law 85–864, pp. 1580–605. Available at: http://tucnak.fsv.cuni.cz/~calda/Documents/1950s/Education_58.html (accessed May 2010).

New Jersey Senate (1978), Education committee hearing, June 20.

No Child Left Behind Act (2001), US Statutes at Large, Public Law 107–110. Available at: http://www2.ed.gov/policy/elsec/leg/esea02/107-110.pdf (accessed May 2010).

Noddings, N. (1994), *A Feminine Approach to Ethics and Moral Education*. London: University of California Press.

Norwood Report (1943), Board of Education, *Curriculum and Examinations in Secondary Schools*. London: HMSO.

Ofsted (2005), *Every Child Matters. The framework for inspection*. London: Ofsted.

Pogosian, V. (2008), Reforms in Russian Education. *International One Day Conference: Innovative Educational Programmes to Build Capacity for Leading Teachers*. Convener A. Taysum. University of Leicester, England, September.

Pring, R. (2005), *Philosophy of Education*. London: Continuum.

Rodriguez, G. (2009), Community collaboration in school improvement. *American Educational Research Association Annual Conference*. San Diego, April.

Rowland, K. (2008), Freedom, inclusion, interaction, and growth: let the children fly: In Taysum, A. (Convener and Chair) *All Children Matter: Addressing Special and Inclusive Education*. Key Note Panel. British Educational Leadership Management, and Administration Society, Aston, July.

Sackett, P., Kuncel, N., Anreson, J., Cooper, S. and Waters, S. (2009), Does socioeconomic status explain the relationship between admission tests and post-secondary academic performance? *Psychology Bulletin*, 135, 1–22.

Sammons, P., Hillman, J. and Mortimore, P. (1995), *Key Characteristics of Effective Schools: a Review of School Effectiveness Research*. A report by the Institute of Education for the Office for Standards in Education.

Shields, C. (2007), A failed initiative: democracy has spoken – or has it? *Journal of Cases in Educational Leadership*, 10 (1), 14–21.

Shields, C., Donmoyer, B., Mohan, E., Ghassan, I., Requa, D., Kose, B. and Taysum, A. (2009), A call for engagement: educational leaders as activists and public intellectuals. *American Educational Research Association Annual Conference*. San Diego, April.

Spring, J. (2008), *American Education*. New York: McGraw Hill.

Springer, M., Herbert, J., Walberg, H., Berends, M. and Ballou, D. (2008), *Handbook of Research on School Choice*. Philadelphia, PA: Lawrence Erlbaum Associates.

Stein. S. (2004), *The Culture of Education Policy*. New York: Teachers College Press, Colombia University.

Strain, M. (1998), Educational managers' knowledge: the quest for useful theory. In

M. Strain, B. Dennison, J. Ouston and V. Hall, *Policy, Leadership and Professional Knowledge in Education*. London: Paul Chapman Publishing.

Taysum, A, (Convener and Chair), Rayner, S., Robertson, C. Farrier and Rowland, K. (2008), All children matter: addressing special and inclusive education. Key Note Panel. *British Educational Leadership, Management and Administration Society Annual Conference*. Aston, July 2008.

Taysum, A. and Gunter, H. (2008), A critical approach to researching social justice and school leadership in England. *Education, Citizenship and Social Justice*, 3 (2), 183–99.

Taysum, A. and Iqbal, M. (2008), An examination of educational policy in England and Pakistan since the Second World War. *British Educational Leadership, Management and Administration Society Annual Conference*. Aston, July 2008.

Taysum, A. (2009), The role of the University in developing educational leaders as public intellectuals through postgraduate research to engage members of minority or marginalized communities and to work on behalf of those least advantaged in society and educational systems. *American Educational Research Association Annual Conference*. San Diego, April 2009.

Taysum, A., Pogosian, V. and Iqbal, M. (2009), Comparing contemporary educational policies in England, The US, Russia and Pakistan; multi-cultural perspectives within the global village. *European Conference for Educational Research*. Vienna, September 2009.

Traxson, D. (2001), De-stressing children in the classroom. In J. Leadbetter, S. Morris, D. Timmins, G. Knight and D. Traxson, *Applying Psychology in the Classroom*. London: David Fulton Publishers.

Troman, G. (2008), Primary teacher identity, commitment and career in performative school cultures. *British Educational Research Journal*, 34 (5), 619–33.

United Nations International Children's Fund (2007), *Child Poverty in Perspective: An overview of child well-being in rich countries*. Florence: The United Nations Children's Fund.

U.S. Department of Education, Office of Elementary and Secondary Education. (2002), *No Child Left Behind: a desktop reference*. Washington, DC.

Wells, A. S. (2008), The social context of charter schools: the changing nature of poverty and what it means for American education. In M. G. Springer, H. J. Walberg, M. Berends and D. Ballou (eds) *Handbook of Research on School Choice*. Philadelphia, PA: Lawrence Erlbaum Associates.

Wells, G. (2003), *Dialogic Inquiry*. Cambridge: Cambridge University Press.

Whitty, G. (2008), Twenty years of progress? English educational policy 1988 to the present. *Educational Management, Administration and Leadership*, 36 (2), 165–84.

Chapter 3

Tools to Facilitate Evidence Informed Leadership

This chapter defines the field that is leadership in education. There is no consensus regarding how to define educational leadership, which is located within a complex field with contested boundaries. This chapter argues that a way of defining leadership in education is to engage with what it feels like for all those involved in that particular leadership within a particular educational community. This means examining how educational leadership may help the formulation of shared understandings within a specific community, which is how identities or personalities are formed (Taysum, 2008). This is particularly important when different agencies from disciplines such as education, health, crime and justice, and social welfare are required to work together with the agenda of Every Child Matters in England and No Child Left Behind in the United States, that seek to remove barriers to social justice.

Discourses about social justice in terms of economic justice and cultural justice are explored. I examine the importance for educational leaders to consider these two elements together rather than treating them as unrelated stand alone issues. I explore how making decisions informed by evidence is important when trying to work for economic and cultural justice. I argue that particular thinking tools may be required to facilitate decision making with a sharp focus on tools that join thinking and doing together to provide empirical evidence for informed educational leadership. The chapter also begins to examine ways such tools may bridge the gap between different groups found in educational settings.

The field of leadership in education

Schools, and by implication educational institutions, are defined by the Oxford English Dictionary (1984) as: 'institution[s] for educating children or giving instruction'. However, there is little agreement of what educational leadership is and how the preparation of future leaders might be organized and developed. Taysum (2008) argues that educational leadership is about the relationships that are built between people in the different phases of education. These relationships engage with the public and the private life of the institution, are situational and are shaped by educational policy. Therefore, educational leadership is shaped by policies that engage with issues of power; that is power to and power over. Ball (2006) argues that such power play, shaped by educational policy is political. Glatter (2009) argues that over the past 15 years educational policies have been driven through with rapid national adoption that stem from good ideas. Glatter asks how do we know a good idea is a good idea, and argues that many educational polices are experiments that are not badged as such. Rather, they are 'hyped up' to ensure 'winning' full adoption, and therefore come with excessive expectations. Glatter (2009) calls this approach: 'big bang' (p. 6). Further, educational policy is open to the economic markets because it is not independent of the state. As Fraser (1997) points out the coupling of the economic and the cultural are played out at a local, national and international level. Here, there are competing systems for a finite amount of resources. Such competitions may occur in the disciplines, or they may occur in the dominant ideology of the day that is set by the elected government of the day (Bates, 2006). The interplay between these processes and markets influences the way(s) in which leadership operates through relationships between all members of the community and the institution. Therefore school leaders potentially include every member of the school community from the national, the district, and the local, the policy maker to learner, from politician to voter, from mayor to parent, and from teacher to governer.

Over time, advocates of models of school leadership (for example, in England, the then Teacher Training Agency, now known as the Teacher Development Agency) have focused on school effectiveness and school improvement. School effectiveness is concerned with outputs whereas school improvement focuses on the processes of school leadership (Macbeath, 2002). Gunter and Rayner (2007) highlight that with English policies such as Every Child Matters, organizational effectiveness and efficiency have dominated the purposes of education, and the kinds of outputs that are in sharp focus are examination results. The league tables that are published position schools according to their examination results but the context of the school is bleached out. This is similar in the States where a policy for No Child Left Behind focuses on examination results, as discussed in Chapter 2. In England, the National College for Leadership of Schools and Children's Services, has effectively licensed headteachers by making it necessary for them to have the National Professional Qualification for Headship. Thrupp (2005) suggests that the licensing of headteachers has a hidden agenda: to transmit educational policy into schools through compliant school leaders. This situation is compounded with the notion of performativity discussed in Chapter 2. Here, the next school initiative is round the corner and there is little time to think about how the last initiative, the current initiative or the initiative to come connects with the values, and needs of the community and its sub-groups.

Values, and the moral ethic are important to civic education and educating for the human *good*, and it is important to examine the community's highest and noblest aims (Collins, 2004). Aristotle (cited in Collins, 2004) speaks of the central role of philosophy for tackling the problems of public and social life, and places the ethical value of an emancipated human as a priority so that they might fully actualize. This argument resonates with Locke's notion of developing moral character (Locke, 1909–14). Arguably on a journey of intellectual, emotional, and spiritual development, where spiritual means the relationship a person has with themselves, a person will need to negotiate being educated, and to use one of Dewey's terms negotiate being 'miseducated' (Pring, 2007). Pring (2007) defines Dewey's experiences of miseducation as those that do not: 'lead to, or which get in the way of, further experiences – which block the mind, as it were, through boredom or fear or indoctrination' (p. 27). Problems in society, coupled with levels of both symbolic violence and physical violence, need solutions that engage with community's highest, and most noble aims. Arguably, what society needs is opportunities for people to tackle the problems of public life, thus society needs the intellectual work of philosophy. Educational leaders need to help teachers do the intellectual work of thinking through how they will approach and engage with problems of public life and social life in their educational institutions and communities. Robertson (2008) argues leaders need to identify leadership potential within their educational communities and develop it, thereby building leadership capacity, and capability. Robertson suggests making safe spaces for dialogue may enable this to start to occur. Taysum (2004) provides evidence that such dialogue gives educational leaders the opportunity to develop shared understanding of how they tackle problems within their own learning communities, and the opportunity to act as critical friends to each other. This has the potential to affect the way in which the practical effects of what educational professionals say to each other about their professional practice is understood, or not. Focusing on the educational journey, rather than the arrival at the destination, moves beyond outcomes-based school effectiveness to connecting school effectiveness with a focus on outcomes with school improvement with a focus on process (Beatty, 2007). Beatty (2007) brings together the notion that: 'School re-culturing is never finished or complete, but rather consists of the myriad of social interactions and evolving relationships that must measure up to new tests every day' (p. 338). Beatty goes on to suggest that opportunities to facilitate collaborative enterprise that is both meaningful and worthwhile is important. Further, Beatty (2007) states it is: 'the personal, social, cultural, and political processes that are shaped and reflected in emotional experiences which will continue to make all the difference' (p. 338). Therefore, leadership that focuses on school renewal needs to be done with humility, honesty, criticality, and, most importantly, in collaboration with all agencies engaged with children's services including education, health, crime and youth justice, and social welfare. Beatty (2007) suggests this will enable the construction of a network of sustainable and strong relationships that can continue to develop and regenerate each other day by day. Problems emerge if there is not enough space and time for educational leaders to think about what they are doing (Taysum, Trapitsin, *et al.*, 2009). The school leaders therefore may not choose to be compliant, they simply may not have time to stop and think. The leaders in my research identified that finding time to stop and think was challenging. Antonia, a former headteacher and current consultant identifies that doing a doctorate made her realize how important it is to be critical and reflective. She realized she needed to stop and think and to make time for this. However, she also identifies that as a manager and a leader in schools, she did not have the thinking time she would have liked. During an interview Antonia said that postgraduate research for a doctorate in Education is important to her because it helped her to:

see things from different perspectives . . . you're more informed. It's a wider perspective and that's always a good thing because if you don't spend time to reflect and to think you get a very tunnel vision, you know, it's like you've always done it that way, or what somebody's said that you must do that. I hope I'll be able to identify irrelevant things and impractical things a little bit more because you're asking questions more about it. But I don't want to be the critical person, the kind of critical, I don't mean critical in the sense that . . . all you do is you're reacting all the time. I want to be critical in a proactive sense . . . I'm going to have to tackle issues to do with power, issues to do with ineffectiveness or effectiveness . . . and then you really get into the more sensitive and delicate areas of work, and I suppose what you're going to say is what are my studies, how is that helping or equipping me to deal with . . . those things. I think what it's doing is giving me a clearer and a better understanding of the complexity of the issue. I think sometimes when you're a manager and a leader managing a school, it's not that you don't actually know, it's because so much is happening and so quickly that you maybe don't analyse enough to plan. You want things done like now and it's a culture, particularly headteachers, find that things have to be done now and it's busy . . . and it's not always the best way of actually getting something done about change.

Hodgson and Spours (2006) identify that thinking time is eroded and they consider there is a lack of political space for critiquing and reflecting upon educational policy and its implementation in educational communities. The lack of critical reflection upon practice may curtail school leaders from moving beyond the government agenda (Rayner *et al.*, 2002) and has the potential to minimize the way in which policy is open to interpretation (Ball, 2006). Campbell *et al.* (2003) critique this position. Their small scale study of six school leaders state the school leaders: 'were able to articulate their values even in the face of government rhetoric exhorting a very different discourse' (p. 128). However, the suggestion is made that to achieve this, school leaders do need time and space to critique and reflect upon practice and become reflexive. This accords with Barnett (1999) who had suggested these elements are essential to develop school leaders' ability to respond appropriately to policy through critique of and reflection upon the policy in their own context. Frameworks for how school leaders might do this have been charted by Gunter (2001) who takes the reader through traits of school leaders, and contingency, transactional and transformational leadership.

Trying to find criteria for defining school leadership is problematic and Strain (1998) argues that leadership may be about constructing what is recognized as meaningful within given situations. These meanings are often affirmed through symbols, objects and rituals. The way they are mediated is also important, and therefore educational leadership might better be understood by how it feels like for all those involved. Here identities are formed as 'good behaviour' is rewarded. The danger here is that behaviour that is not deemed wanted by the dominant group may be ignored. Bates (2006) recalls the 'perfectability' of Nazis and fascism idealism, and this timely reminder serves to demonstrate that the dominant group may be committing evil crimes against humanity. Challenge to this ideology is essential but the dominant group might try to ignore it and misrecognize the challengers. Misrecognition may take many forms, with consequences ranging from the terrible horrors caused by Nazism to the kind of misrecognition Shields (2007) refers to in Chapter 2. Educational leaders doing postgraduate research that I interviewed expressed that they had been misrecognized in one way or another. One headteacher described she was misrecognized as a woman in a male-dominated way of thinking about and doing leadership in schools. As stated previously, pseudonyms have been provided in the following quotation in the interests of anonymity and confidentiality. Hannah states:

> The doctorate certainly made me question my perception of who and what I was and as I say, how can I describe that? It became very much a case in the way that things were analysed that women who had been appointed to headship at about the same time as me, or before me and had young children, they tend to share my perceptions. It was a male dominated approach to leadership. It was the do I actually have a right to be the headteacher because after all I am a woman and have got children and you know, please may I be a headteacher, instead of well actually I've a right to be a headteacher and I have skills and attributes that are quite valuable in this situation. Women who are younger and who had been appointed much more recently had an entirely different view of headship.

Thus school leaders have the power to recognize or misrecognize their own contribution to an educational community and that of others within the community. This power needs careful thinking about, but as I argued earlier it is not always possible to think about the practice of leadership, if the time and space is not provided in the very busy educational environment. The implications of this kind of power make evidence informed leadership even more important because identities are being formed. Thus it might be argued that school leadership is moving towards being defined by the way it is collectively understood by all those affected by it regardless of local, national and international contexts. Understanding educational leadership is therefore important because it engages with the construction of knowledge over time and shapes identities.

The formation of identities

Throughout Western history there have been contests over knowledge as science and knowledge as culture. Putting it simply, scientific knowledge might be that found in the university, and cultural knowledge might be that co-constructed by practitioners. Trying to work out which kind of knowledge is important and how different kinds of knowledges might be presented for acquisition within educational communities is important. Each different kind of knowledge will probably have an interest group within society's infrastructure that will champion it, and lobby for its inclusion in the curriculum. Yet some groups have more power than others. This may lead to discrimination, marginalization and minoritization, which creates barriers to economic justice, cultural justice and the opportunity to associate democratically in the negotiation of a culturally and economically relevant curriculum as referred to earlier. Those that have financial power may be able to influence educational policy makers, while recognizing the importance of other groups who may not be as 'cash rich'. Yet equally there may be some wealthy stakeholders within society who do not recognize forms of knowledge beyond their own, and may work actively to exclude forms of knowledge that do not fit their agenda.

Clearly, this has significant implications for the notion of curriculums and the extent to which the construction of a curriculum within an educational community might be shared. Delanty (2001) calls such sharing of knowledge access, use, and transformation 'the democratization of knowledge'. Yet there are barriers to this process taking place, because members of a community need to acquire tools to reach a provisional and just consensus in decision making surrounding what is included in a curriculum and what is left out. Indeed Plato, summed up by Delanty (2001), argues: 'knowledge and democracy are incompatible and that nothing can bridge the worlds of the cave and the academy' (p. 1). It is important to gain the right tools to be able to reach just decisions about curriculum-building before such decisions can be made. However, if dominant groups do not want members of educational communities to have the power to build their own curriculums, then they need only prevent them from gaining the tools to do so. To that end there have always been ontological (what is) and epistemological (the knowledge of what is) struggles within the infrastructure of society with the highest of stakes to play for. The stakes are high in these contests because they are contextualized within political struggles about the individual and her/his relationship with the infrastructure s/he inhabits.

The struggles therefore are about the distribution of power between individuals, infrastructures and by implication the taken-for-grantedness or in other words 'the dominant discourses' of the day. This is demonstrated by Taysum (2006), who cites Mahoney and Winterer's (2002) argument that university curriculums have historically:

> trained a socially and politically powerful elite in the arts of rhetoric, logic and semantics; well into the early modern period, classical learning was a highly vocational education, though it also bestowed a patina of cultural prestige. (p. 518)

The education and training enabled the elite to take positions of power and authority and sustain the taken-for-granted views of the day. The dominant discourses or hegemony influenced the structures that shaped what people could and could not do – or their 'agency', positioning the elite to continue to access and possess the necessary capital in its various forms (Bourdieu, 2000). Bourdieu (2000) suggests there are four forms of captial. The first is economic capital which is based on fiscal issues. The second is social capital which is won through valuable relationships with significant others. The third is cultural capital won by having legitimate knowledge which may be gained through competences or subject areas. Finally, symbolic capital is won through social honour and status. This enabled the elite to maintain their status as elites from generation to generation. Access to the required capital maintained the elites' positions of power and authority while excluding those without the required capital from accessing such positions of power and authority. Thus, the elite status remained unchallenged and the curriculums they engaged with enabled them to socially construct a taken-for-granted way of knowing and doing (Bourdieu, 2000). The social-constructs are therefore deeply embedded in the psyche of citizens and can be affirmed and re-affirmed from generation to generation in what might be described as a deterministic way (Bourdieu, 2000). Such shared understanding has the appearance of being natural, and people may believe they are being authentic. However, the foundations on which their belief systems are built may not be authentic. These concepts will be explored further in Chapter 4. Suffice to say that the art and science of teaching work and activity, or pedagogic work and activity was led through language, and shared meanings by those who legitimized language, symbols and meanings among people. Such work and activity forms the identities of citizens and the structures that structure their agency within a society. It is arguably important for agents to begin to critique pedagogic work and activity, to reveal how they may have taken-for-granted their career and life choices that have shaped their career and life trajectories. Beginning to ask the 'why' questions may illuminate alternative futures that were hitherto hidden. Different language might be used for old practices that enable people to think about the common sense view in different ways. For example, changing the label 'chairman' to 'chair' may help women see that serving as a 'chair' or 'chairperson' is work for a woman or a man. Alternative futures of this kind may have an improved chance of being built on foundations that are authentic and will facilitate human behaviour being authentic. Such critiquing is potentially emancipatory and may identify and stimulate the removal of barriers to social justice. Once recognition of these barriers occurs, agents may have windows of opportunity to make more informed choices about how to respond to them. These ideas are summed up by Strain (1998), who states:

Recalling the 'critical role' accorded to followers of Max Weber, Gronn most persuasively cites 'an emerging consensus that leading is an inherently symbolic activity', an activity imbued with the intrinsically human capacity to frame meaning, 'to make sense of one's own and others' experiences of the world'. If leadership activities are to contribute as we would wish to the construction of a shared social reality, support of the group must be mobilized through exchange of shared symbols and meanings. This is how *identities* are formed. (p. 23)

Therefore, symbolic systems are created where social reality is not being shaped by elements external to individuals. Rather, social reality is constructed by internal elements that people shape through doing things habitually. Reality is *objectified* by citizens who construct it, externalize this knowledge and so define their reality accordingly (Taysum, 2006). Carr and Kemmis (2002) affirm this by suggesting that social reality and social order are constructed by recogniz-ing systems of meanings that are construed and re-construed (Senge, 1997) by the members of the society. Those not given the chance to contribute to the construction of knowledge, are excluded from the creation of symbolic systems, and therefore making a 'reality' which they can play an equal part in. Such a blockade is a barrier to democracy and social justice.

Taysum (2006) argues that excluding citizens from knowledge creation has the potential to impact a country's financial position and cites Brooks and Mackinnon (2001) argument that knowledge is a resource for developing a country's economic wealth. If education is important to the wealth of a nation, then unpacking the relationship between knowledge and the economy is impor-tant. Taysum (2006) cites Brooks and Mackinnon (2001) argument that the income or patent that knowledge might provide is a commodity. Further, income generated from a knowledge economy has the potential to make a country more competitive in a global economy (Taysum, 2006). The economic element is clear but this needs to be balanced with the cultural element (Fraser, 1997).

Cultural capital is rooted predominantly in the possession of legitimate knowledge (Bourdieu, 2000) Having access to the right kinds of tools that would enhance the individual's legitimate knowledge can establish and develop their fluency in negotiating symbolic systems (Taysum, 2006a). An individual's ability to co-create the symbolic structures is heightened by their economic and cultural capital which positioned them so that they might privilege their way of knowing and doing over others. Thus the emergent dominant epistemology (the knowledge of what is) and the dominant ontology (what is) can be developed, sustained and labelled *a common sense view of reality*. Ironically such a way of knowing and doing is anything but common since it is designed and perpetuated by the dominant few that understand the mechanics of it. Yet it spreads to citizens who do not hold the legitimate knowledge that underpins the common sense view, such that they believe the common sense view without having any notion of the commonality or lack of commonality of the legitimate knowledge, because they do not possess it. The need for evidence informed practice that enables people to examine the common sense view, and from their revelations make informed decisions within an articulated ethical framework becomes clearer. However, those that are dominant in the development of the common sense view may not wish people to be critical or reflective because it may threaten their dominance.

Educational leadership facilitating shared understandings through evidence informed practice within an ethical framework

Using empirical evidence from systematic and rigorous postgraduate research has the potential to enable practitioners to penetrate the symbolic systems that may constrain what they can and can not know and do, or their 'agency'. Moreover, those who engage with evidence informed leadership can offer windows of opportunities to other members of their communities to begin to engage with evidence informed leadership. This has the potential to enable practitioners to gain insights into different ways of knowing and doing. Arguably this frees individuals from objective structures in the field that had previously shaped their mental models, enabling them to make more informed choices about the ways in which their subjective expectations might meet their objective chances (Bourdieu, 2000). With this reframing of mental models, agency moves beyond being structured by deterministic closed systems generated by the few with legitimate knowledge. Rather agents have the potential to gain insight into the ways in which they might work for change within open systems. This gives glimpses into ways in which working for change might begin to remove barriers to social justice and shows that educational leaders might foster what Delanty (2001, p. 6) calls 'the democratization of knowledge' and what Bourdieu (2000, p. 65) calls 'communicative action'.

Shared understanding is important with different agencies from children's services with the agenda of Every Child Matters and No Child Left Behind

Sharing understanding is entwined with the share of power between different agencies from different disciplines with the agenda of Every Child Matters and No Child Left Behind. Dowding (1996) suggests 'power to' can be described as outcome power which 'is the ability of an actor to bring about or help to bring about outcomes' (p. 5). Power to may involve cooperation and 'power over' seems to involve conflict (Dowding, 1996). Clearly the kinds of joined-up thinking that might occur between different agencies is key to understanding whether strategies of cooperation or conflict are being deployed within an educational institution. When thinking about cooperation Bennett *et al.* (2003) suggest that distributing leadership throughout an institution is a helpful way of thinking through how to engage with leadership. How we may begin to conceptualize this is provided by Harris (2004) when she argues that distributed leadership engages educational professionals to develop expertise by working collaboratively within an organization that may transcend formal positions or roles.

This is in contrast to designer leaders who have a checklist of standards that embed conflict between the self and the environment within which the leader operates (Gronn, 2003). This linear construct limits the agency of players within the structures they operate in. Gronn (2003) continues:

[H]istoric patterns of voluntarist, pluralistic identity construction are yielding to centralized, monocultural norm imposition and forms of standardization that de-legitimate and minimize variations of personal career passage. (p. 71)

This designer leadership resonates with the notion of 'the power of one' (Harris, 2002). Where the leader presents a vision for the school and the followers follow it. The leader may have a vision and aspirations for the school. However as Earley *et al.* (2002) suggest: 'Being unable to live up to their own and others' expectations may be a key factor which leads to demotivation and stress' (p. 44). Designer leaders can influence the culture of a school and empower people to say and do as they are told through bases of power. The combination therefore of the institutional focus, structural focus and behavioural focus (Dowding, 1996) interwoven with bases of power (French and Raven, 1968) and identification of resources on which to draw may put a constraint on, or increase creativity within an educational institution.

Stoll *et al.* (2003) suggest that community dialogue enables a shared sense of meaning: 'about where you are going as a school and working to adapt your goals in the light of messages from your context' (p. 142). Such dialogue could open up discussion around what Hall (1997) calls 'confronting the taken for granted . . . where understanding leaders and managers in education means understanding them as people' (p. 312). Therefore, understanding educational leadership means understanding the behaviour and the intent for that behaviour. Space needs to be created to enable members of different agencies to engage in dialogue to share understandings of how to meet the Every Child Matters and No Child Left Behind policy agendas in their particular context. This is important because Southworth (2004) suggests dialogue can shape and develop practice. Engaging with such discourses has the potential to enable community-based learning to happen where discourses about social justice in terms of economic justice and cultural justice might occur (Taysum and Gunter, 2008). Community-based learning or place-based learning, or 'place-conscious education' introduces students to the skills and dispositions needed to make healthy contributions to the community both economically and culturally so that their communities are sustainable. Greunewald and Smith (2008) argue this is important and that a part of the learners' education should be drawn from 'local phenomena'. This helps shared understandings to be developed as the learners associate with the local and particular. Co-constructing curriculums is in contrast to an imposed curriculum that presents standardized knowledge that is potentially alien to the lived experiences of the learners. Before thinking through how community-based learning might facilitate real and meaningful engagement with social justice agendas it is important to think through what is meant by social justice.

Discourses about economic and cultural social justice and the implications for community-based learning

It is both meaningful and worthwhile for all those considering the Every Child Matters and No Child Left Behind agendas to come to some provisional consensus of what is meant by social justice in terms of equity. Equity might be defined as redistributing resources differentially to groups who are the most disadvantaged in terms of poverty. Cribb and Gewirtz (2003) framework of social justice is useful to think through issues of equity. The social justice framework was introduced in Chapter 2 to theorize how students' parents may be democratically involved in the co-construction of knowledge in schools and colleges. Cribb and Gewirtz (2003) three key considerations of the social justice framework will now be used to begin to theorize the context of groups that are the least advantaged in society. As stated in Chapter 2 the first is distributive, second is cultural and third is associational. Distributive refers to economic justice where consideration needs to be given to groups who have been exploited, marginalized, and deprived (Fraser, 1997). I will look at these three terms in turn. First, exploitation can be understood as the gains from human work, including child labour, that are redistributed to those who are not part of the labour process. Bourdieu (1998) argues that this practice leaves those being exploited disillusioned, with a poor self-image. The lack of confidence in itself may prevent people from challenging the way they are positioned in society, and in the labour market, and may stop them from recognizing what an education system can offer them (Howe, 1997). Their education may be experienced passively where external motivation to pass tests is something that is done to them so that education might foster a kind of learned helplessness. This is in sharp contrast to the student leading their learning and having a balance of being both internally motivated and externally motivated that might foster an ethical disposition for civic work. The second is economic marginalization. Those experiencing economic marginalization may have no job, or if they do have a job it may be very poorly paid. The final category is deprivation where the material standard of living is inadequate and often illegal, and this might be referred to as absolute poverty. On the surface different groups may appear to be treated equally, yet the differences between the groups when working towards the equalizing of resources is not addressed. Bates (2006) argues it is important to give resources to the least advantaged. Internationally this might also be understood in terms of the distribution of aid when working towards Millennium Development Goals of 2015 (United Nations, 2009).

The second consideration of Cribb and Gewirtz is cultural justice and they develop this concept by citing Fraser (1997) who argues that cultural domination is important for the transmission of socially constructed discourses. For cultural justice to exist, there needs to be respect and, at best, an unconditional positive regard for difference that operates within ethical frameworks, and at worst, a tolerance for difference that operates within ethical frameworks. Working for change that seeks to move sub-groups of communities, particularly the least advantaged towards a situation where all cultures are recognized and respected may be one way of removing barriers to social justice.

The final consideration within Cribb and Gewirtz's (2003) conceptualization is that of the associational where spaces are created for all members of a community to contribute to a democratic decision making process so that they can associate with the rules and ethical frameworks that shape what they can and can not do. Dialogue may be a way forward here, but it needs to be evidence informed if it is to be meaningful and worthwhile. Thus converting written policy into practice needs to be done collaboratively, but also needs to be evidence informed.

Evidence informed leadership for communities

Those who lead schools, arguably headteachers and senior leaders, are in receipt of policies that are developed away from the location within which they are to be realized. The policy as text is constructed so that there is little room for interpretation other than how the policy writers wanted it to be interpreted. Ball (2006) illuminates this:

> Policy authors do make concerted efforts to assert such control by the means
> at their disposal, to achieve a 'correct' reading and some texts are framed by
> or have embedded the weight, and measure, or requirement. (p. 44)

As previously stated, policies are political, and Ball (2006) argues the process of
policy formation can be random, or lucky. Randomness and luck are not part of a
systematic and rigorous approach to policy making that educational communities
can learn to systematically and democratically engage with. In short it might be
argued that 'randomness and luck' are not the stuff of ethical civic work. Freire
(1972) argues that leaders need to be involved in the writing of policy so that they
can develop the knowledge, thinking tools, and experience required to develop
policy that is meaningful to their particular communities. Moreover, leaders may
be able to facilitate cultural groups within their communities to co-construct writing policy, and the operationalization of policy. Such policy work is what Gandin
and Apple (2002) and Furman and Greunewald (2004) call community-based
education. Community-based education has the potential to give community
members more control over how they experience their lives, and how they recognize and celebrate the diversities of their different cultures. The community may
choose the themes that they want to explore, and their teachers may take these
themes and use them to tune into how to make the acquisition of literacy and
numeracy skills more meaningful (Corson, 1998). Finding different 'ways in' to
reach individuals' internal motivation to learn something is important. This kind
of pedagogic work can only take place when relationships have been developed
and the teachers have begun to recognize what themes may be of interest to different members of the community. Community-based learning may also foster
the coupling of economic and culture justice through facilitating a community's
association with the rules and structures that shape their members' identities
(Gandin and Apple, 2002; Thomson, 2006). Evidence informed leadership of
communities who collaborate in the writing, operationalization and leadership
of policies as text and discourse (Ball, 2006) may be emancipatory and contribute
to the removal of barriers to social justice. Developing self-awareness is important to
facilitate evidence informed leadership, and thinking tools may be required
to facilitate evidence informed leadership as a way to bridge the gap between the
different groups in educational settings.

Conclusions

To sum up, defining leaderships in education is complex but it may be understood by how it feels like for all those involved. This means examining how educational leadership may facilitate the formulation of shared understandings, which is how identitites are formed. This is particularly important when different agencies from disciplines such as education, health, crime and justice, and social welfare are required to work together with the agenda of Every Child Matters and No Child Left Behind that seeks to remove barriers to social justice. Economic and cultural injustice may be embedded if educational policies do not recognize cultural difference (Bourdieu, 2000). Thinking tools such as critical analysis, reflection and the ability to be reflexive may help practitioners develop evidence informed leadership. An important part of this process is developing self-awareness. Such tools may help learners to understand the interplay between what shapes what they can and can not do and the power issues involved. This may free them up from structures that are constraining, which is arguably liberating. It is argued that ways of joining thinking and enterprise for the betterment of communities in educational settings need to be found.

The next chapter explores what evidence informed leadership might contribute to communities in educational settings to better understand themselves, how this might lead to building civic responsibility, and the time and tools potentially needed to achieve this.

References

Ball, S. J. (2006), *Education Policy and Social Class*. London: Routledge.

Barnett, R. (1999), *Realizing the University in an Age of Supercomplexity*. Buckingham: Open University Press.

Bates, R. (2006), Presidential address: public education, social justice and teacher education. *Asia-Pacific Journal of Teacher Education*, 34 (3), 275–86.

Beatty, B. (2007), 'Going through the emotions: leadership that gets to the heart of school renewal', *Australian Journal of Education*, 51 (3), 328–40.

Bennett, N., Wise, C., Woods, P. and Harvey, J. (2003), *Distributed Leadership: A review of literature*. National College for School Leadership.

Bourdieu, P. (1998), *Acts of Resistance Against the Tyranny of the Market, 2*. New York: The New Press.

Bourdieu, P. (2000), *Pascalian Meditations*. Cambridge: Polity.

Brooks, F. and Mackinnon, M. (2001), *Gender and the Restructured University*. Buckingham: Open University Press.

Campbell, C., Gold, A. and Lunt, I. (2003), Articulating leadership values in action: conversations with school leaders. *International Journal of Leadership in Education*, 6 (3), 203–21.

Carr, W. and Kemmis, S. (2002), *Becoming Critical*. London: Falmer Press.

Collins, S. (2004), Moral virtue and the limits of the political community in Artistotle's Nichomachean Ethics. *American Journal of Political Science*, 48 (1), 47–61.

Corson, D. (1998), *Changing Education for Diversity*. Buckingham: Open University Press.

Cribb, A. and Gewirtz, S. (2003), Towards a sociology of just practices; an analysis of plural conceptions of justice. In C. Vincent (ed.), *Social Justice Education and Identity* (pp. 15–29). London: RoutledgeFalmer.

Delanty, G. (2001), *Challenging Knowledge: The university in the knowledge society*. Buckingham: SRHE/Open University Press.

Dowding, K. (1996), *Power*. Buckingham: Open University Press.

Earley, P., Evans, J., Collarbone, P., Gold, A. and Halpin, D. (2002), *Establishing the Current State of School Leadership in England*. Available from http://www.dfes.gov.uk/research/data/uploadedfiles/RR336pdf (accessed 15 December 2005).

Fraser, N. (1997), *Justice Interruptus: Critical reflections on the 'postsocialist' condition*. London: Routledge.

Freire, P. (1972), *Pedagogy of the Oppressed*. Harmondsworth: Penguin.

French, R. and Raven, J. (1968), The bases of social power. In D. Cartwright and A. Zander (eds), *Group Dynamics*. Wiltshire: Tavistock Publications.

Furman, C. and Greunewald, A. (2004), Expanding the landscape of social justice: a critical and ecological analysis. *Education Administration Quarterly*, 40 (1), 47–76.

Gandin, L. and Apple, M. (2002), Challenging neo-liberalism building a democracy: creating the citizen school in Porto Alegre Brazil. *Journal of Education Policy*, 17 (2), 259–79.

Glatter, R. (2009), The governance of education: current challenges. *Management in Education*, 15, (2), 6–9.

Grace, G. (1995), *School Leadership Beyond Education Management: An essay in policy scholarship*. London: The Falmer Press.

Gronn, P. (2003), *The New Work of Educational Leaders*. London: Sage.

Greunewald, D. and Smith. G. (2008), *Place-Based Education in the Global Age: Local diversity*. New York: Lawrence Erlbaum.

Gunter, H. (2001), *Leaders and Leadership in Education*. London: Paul Chapman.

Gunter, H. M. and Rayner, S. (2007), Modernising the school workforce in England: challenging transformation and leadership? *Leadership*, 3 (1), 47–64.

Hall, V. (1997), Dusting off the phoenix. Gender and educational leadership revisited. *Educational Management and Administration*, 25 (3), 309–24.

Harris, A. (2002), Distributed Leadership in Schools: Leading or Misleading. Key Note Paper presented at the *British Educational Leadership Management and Administration Society Annual Conference*. Birmingham, England.

Harris, A. (2004), Distributed leadership in schools: leading or misleading? *Management in Education*, 16 (10), 10–13.

Hodgson, A. and Spours, K. (2006), An analytical framework for policy engagement: 'the contested case of 14–19 reforms in England'. *Journal of Education Policy*, 21 (6).

Howe, K. (1997), *Understanding Equal Education Opportunity. Social justice democracy and schooling*. London: Falmer.

Jarvis, P. (2000), The changing university: meeting a need and needing to change. *Higher Education Quarterly*, 54 (2), 43–67.

Locke, J. (1909–14), *Some Thoughts Concerning Education*, (ed.) C. W. Eliot. The Harvard Classics, Vol. XXXVII, Part 1. New York: P. F. Collier & Son.

Macbeath. J. (2002), Leadership, learning, and the challenge to democracy. In Walker, A. and Dimmock, C. (eds), S*chool Leadership and Administration. Adopting a cultural perspective.* New York: RoutledgeFalmer.

Mahoney, K. and Winterer, C. (2002). The problem of the past in the modern university: Catholics and Classicists, 1860–1900. *History of Education Quarterly*, 43 (4), 517–543.

Pring, R. (2007), *John Dewey a Philosopher of Education for Our Time?* London: Continuum.

Rayner, S., Gunter, H. M. and Powers, S. (2002), Professional development needs for leaders in special education. *Journal of In-Service Education*, 28 (1), 79–93.

Robertson, J. (2008), *Coaching Educational Leadership Building Capacity through Partnership.* London: Sage.

School, N. (1984), *The Oxford English Dictionary.* Oxford: Oxford University Press.

Shields, C. (2007), A failed initiative: democracy has spoken – or has it? *Journal of Cases in Educational Leadership*, 10 (1), 14–21.

Southworth, G. (2004). *Primary School Leadership in Context: Leading small, medium and large sized schools.* London: RoutledgeFalmer.

Stoll, L., Fink, D. and Earl, L. (2003), *It's About Learning (and It's About Time): What's in it for schools?* London: RoutledgeFalmer.

Strain, M. (1998), Educational managers' knowledge: the quest for useful theory. In M. Strain, B. Dennison, J. Ouston and V. Hall, *Policy, Leadership and Professional Knowledge in Education.* London: Paul Chapman Publishing.

Sykes, J. B. (1984), *Oxford English Dictionary.* Oxford: Clarendon Press.

Taysum, A. (2004), Critical perspectives on leading and managing schools to improve teaching and learning: finding space for middle management to build dialogue to improve teaching and learning. *BELMAS SCRELM Research Conference New Understandings in Educational Leadership and Management.* St Catherine's Oxford University.

Taysum, A. (2006a), *A Survey of the Learning Journeys of School Leaders doing the Doctorate of Education in England.* Birmingham: University of Birmingham.

Taysum, A. (2006b), The distinctiveness of the EdD within the university tradition. *Journal of Education Administration and History*, 38 (3), 323–34.

Taysum, A. (2008), The role of research in developing educational leadership for the 21st century. *American Educational Research Association Annual Conference.* New York, USA.

Taysum, A. and Gunter, H. (2008), A critical approach to researching social justice and school leadership in England. *Education, Citizenship and Social Justice*, 3 (2), 183–199.

Taysum, A., Trapitsin, S., Shah, S., Gromova, L., Mercer, J. and Pushkinova, E. (2009), How educational leaders learn to mediate complex policy contexts: co-constructing evidence based practice in partnership with English and Russian Higher Education Institutions. *Society for the Furtherance of Critical Philosophy Annual Conference*, Chichester, July.

Thomson, P. (2006), Miners, diggers, ferals and showmen: school-community projects that affirm and unsettle identities and place. *British Journal of Sociology of Education*, 27 (1), 81–96.

Thomson, J. (2004), *Aristotle: The Nicomachean Ethics.* London: Penguin Books.

Thrupp, M. (2005), The National College for School Leadership: a critique. *Management in Education*, 19 (2), 13–19.

United Nations (2009), United Nations Millennium Development Goals. Available from: http://www.un.org/millenniumgoals/ accessed 9 26, 2009. http://www.portalus.ru/modules/ruseconomics/rus_readme.php?subaction=showfull&id=1162193464&archive=&start_from=&ucat=16&category=16 (accessed 26 September 2009).

Chapter 4

Moving Towards Shared Understandings in Complex Educational Settings

This chapter explores how evidence informed leadership might contribute to communities in educational settings moving towards understanding themselves, each other and their role regarding civic work. A new grammar of thinking is introduced and the potentially false dichotomy between theory and practice is exposed and the notion of praxis is carefully explained and contextualized. An explanation of what is meant by epistemology (the knowledge of what is) and ontology (what is) in simple English is also presented. I also consider why it is important to explain what is meant by epistemology and ontology and why different 'ways of knowing' or 'epistemological approaches' are vital for evidence informed leadership.

Developing leaders for evidence informed leadership through postgraduate research

Engaging with postgraduate research (PGR) has the potential to develop educational leaders for a complex and rapidly changing educational system that is located within an equally challenging international context. Doing postgraduate research arguably equips educational leaders for evidence informed leadership so that important decisions can be made when handling educational policy. To make decisions informed by evidence the evidence needs to be reliable, systematic and trustworthy. Lunt (2002), Hall (1998), Bowden, Bourner and Laing (2002) and Scott *et al.* (2004) suggest that postgraduate research develops rigorous researchers and consumers of research while respecting the knowledge and expertise of the educational professional. Taysum (2007b) supports this argument and cites Biddle and Saha (2005) who conducted research with 120 school principals in the United States and found doing educational research shaped the leaders' thinking. Thus postgraduate research under-pinned evidence informed leadership. Taysum, (2007b) rehearses that Crow (2004) suggests research is excluded from the development of leaders and argues: 'the important development of leaders rarely includes research in the USA' (p. 297). An important research project called 'The Carnegie Initiative on the Doctorate' (CID) looked at six disciplines over a five-year period, including education, to try to further understand the influence of research upon each of the disciplines. The findings revealed that there is a place for postgraduate research, and that the doctorate should prepare stewards of the field (Golde, 2006). However, there are arguments against some kinds of postgraduate research (Taysum, 2007b). Levine (2005) suggests masters programmes may be beneficial for school leaders and cites the Master of Educational Administration, but he argues that the Educational Doctorate (EdD) is not helpful. Yet, Shulman *et al.* (2006) argue that trying to prepare practitioners and scholars through postgraduate teaching/pedagogy may be worthwhile because a grammar of thinking is developed that can be applied in untested situations in schools. This means that the educational leader might approach difficult decision making with a kind of a 'preparedness' provided by a logical and meaningful way of thinking (Taysum, 2007b). Such decision making moves beyond a manager who leads using a manual where solutions are learned and copied. Copying solutions from a one size fits all manual limits authentic association with the solution to a problem. Moreover, such tools are limited to the tried and tested problems that are held within the pages. These solutions may or may not contain just or unjust solutions. The danger here is that unless the decision maker reads the prescribed solutions critically, they may make a decision based on the prescribed models that accidentally further embed inequalities. Thus their solutions might add to the problems rather than solve them. Ironically, if the leader does read the solutions critically, then there is an argument that they do not need the prescribed solutions in the first place because they have the necessary tools to collect evidence in situ and make an evidence informed judgement. However, what is more troubling is that the prescribed solutions presented in a leadership manual may not be based in evidence. Rather the solutions may be fictional or anecdotal to suit the purpose of the writer of the manual. Such management that is copied, lacks authentic intellectual work made by real people for real people. Intellectual work, and the inherent and transparent democratic processes that give it the hallmark of authentic intellectual work may be the stuff of civic work. By this I mean, habitually making evidence informed decisions that are arrived at through democratic public intellectual work may develop and affirm dispositions within communities that may lead to communities that enjoy civic responsibility. The desire for civic responsibility may be internally motivated and may be arrived at through leaders who are committed to evidence informed leadership themselves. In this way the leader might be what John Locke calls a wise person, who both develops and role models good habits (Locke, 1909–14). Habitually making decisions in this way may lead to moment-to-moment authentic decision making. This may flow between the science and art of pedagogy or pedagogic work (Luke, 2006). Such democratic authentic evidence informed leadership might be found in relationships between the various members of an educational community, and the processes or structures that enable this to happen smoothly.

To think through the journey from copying to becoming authentic, Eraut (1994, cites Broudy *et al.*, 1964) views the shift from reproduction to authenticity in stages. These stages are called 'modes of knowledge' in the context of Continuing Professional Education. The four modes here are: replication; application; interpretation; and association. The first and second modes of replication and application are not helpful and Eraut demonstrates this with regard to teachers. Eraut suggests the complexities of teaching do not enable copying or simply applying the guidelines of a teacher's manual to develop good practice. However, Eraut (1994) does perceive the interpretation mode to be useful. This is because he argues that to interpret the ideas or theories presented, learners must internalize the ideas or theories. This means that they will need to explore how the theories might connect with what is important to them, or their values. It will also call upon them to explore any emerging value conflicts to support what is right (Gunter, 2005). Arguably it will take courage for educational leaders to apply these concepts of internalizing theories and exploring emerging value conflicts in their practice (Shields *et al.*, 2009). Further, if the leaders are able to engage in this kind of public intellectual work, how do the leaders choose from the myriad of theories available? This question is further problematized when consideration is given to the fourth mode, that of the associational. Eraut suggests that how knowledge is related to, or associated with is very important. The association may be evidence informed as I have been considering in the first three chapters. However, the association might be developed out of a series of memories. This is illustrated using Eraut's example of a series of memories that a teacher may have of a child. Eraut (1994) states:

> A teacher's store of information about a child is like a collection of film-clips, each clip portraying a separate incident, usually fairly brief but rich in contextual detail. Thinking about the child involves reviewing some of these clips, and records . . . when one then compares a standardized test-score to a single still picture and a record card to a stereotyped film review, the impossibilities of producing a short summary of a child's abilities and progress becomes obvious. (p. 28)

Eraut further suggests that this process of associating may link to a community member's disposition that has not been developed to recognize democratic and evidence-informed decision making that is exercised with a commitment to an ongoing development of self-awareness. Rather, the process of association might draw on a person's anecdotal experience where the strong influence of their personality on their practice is not recognized or questioned. Eraut proposes that continuing professional development works best when it opens windows for educational professionals to *explore* their mental models, to get to know themselves better. This means thinking through and critically reflecting upon the way in which they experience the internalizing of theories and/or the way in which they associate with particular ways of thinking or behaving. This kind of activity focuses on trying to understand the self better and is important identity work. Such critical reflection may reveal that a person has unintentionally been racist, or experienced some kind of prejudice that they had not realized was unjust. *Challenging* these ways of thinking and doing is potentially uncomfortable. For Delanty (2001) and Freire (1972) this kind of intellectual work is very important, and may enable professional educationalists to develop the thinking tools needed to facilitate the critique of theories so that they can make more informed choices regarding their evidence informed leadership and how to best work with and for the communities they serve.

Flessa (2007) argues that the intellectual endeavour required of postgraduate research is important for the development of educational leaders. To get to the point of ethical and good decision making, the intellectual work involved includes educational leaders reading different authoritative perspectives from the substantive literature on their particular topic. The different viewpoints from potentially diverse contexts enable the reader to look at their own particular topic with refreshed eyes, while preventing the reinvention of the wheel. Such systematic critical analysis needs to be evidence informed. This is where the peer review process is important because it provides a gate keeping service for knowledge. Through peer review, knowledge that is published has met minimum standards that deem it to be meaningful, worthwhile and evidence informed. When leaders access knowledge that is trustworthy, the reader can compare or contrast the different views, or 'critically analyse' the literature. This intellectual work may be the key to unlocking that which keeps them in the grip of their current situation. As they think through their problem in different ways, they are potentially able to come back to their own ethical decision-making process, and objectify the extent to which it is evidence informed. The minimum standards discussed here are reflected in criteria of doctoral postgraduate research as provided by the Quality Assurance Authority (QAA, 2007):

> Holders of doctoral degrees will have the qualities needed for employment that require both the ability to make informed judgements on complex issues in specialist fields and an innovative approach to tackling and solving problems. (pp. 24–5)

Therefore, postgraduate research curriculums have at their heart what might be labelled a moral and noble imperative to impart ways of thinking and doing that will facilitate evidence informed leadership. Postgraduate research programme providers may work at the centre of a network of leaders engaging with postgraduate research. The programme provider's role may be one of supervision as they guide the postgraduate research student through the substantive literature relevant to their chosen topic, and provide tools for students to engage in their own reviews. The programme provider may also provide training and education in research methods and present the rich methodological literature to the postgraduate research student. Students can then choose to carry out research as knowledge workers, users and transformers with the potential of becoming a public intellectual who in turn can become a gatekeeper of the field. Taysum (2008) argues that this conforms to the QAA published criteria of doctoral level qualifications:

> Doctorates are awarded for the creation and interpretation of knowledge, which extends the forefront of the discipline, usually through original research. Holders of research will be able to conceptualize, design and implement projects for the generation of significant new knowledge and/or understanding. (QAA, 2008)

When generating new knowledge, the postgraduate researchers may engage with issues of power within their communities, thus they will engage with the political, social, cultural and economic elements. Postgraduate researchers will need to think about their own position within power relationships between the activities of their communities and the various structures that bound those activities, such as legislation. This is particularly important if they hold privileged positions of leadership. When considering issues of power, the postgraduate researcher will need to think through the importance of histories that have brought agents to where they are now. This kind of knowing engages with understanding the self and embraces the important concept of what Socrates called 'know yourself inscribed [*sic*] at the temple at Delphi', cited in Beck (2003).

It is important for leaders to 'know the self' as a rich, complex human being who is a leader on a physical, intellectual, emotional, and spiritual level. To do this the leader needs to consider the way they think and the way they behave. This may be thought of in terms of cognitive learning styles, which Riding and Rayner (2005) suggest may be present at birth and are relatively fixed. However, the environment also influences a person's mental models such as the 'societal norms' of the time, or the 'generational norms/cohort factors', the primary carers, and the culture of the person (Taysum, 2003). Understanding these kinds of influences sheds light on how and why the self has been constructed. This is particularly important when understanding the culture and values of an educational community and how these shape the identities of the members of the community. Duffy (1999) describes how: 'I was perceived as "the head" – a separate entity from my "self" – a "construct"' (p. 107). Developing a profound awareness of how such a projected construct threads its way in and out of the leader's sense of identity is to know the self. Earlier, I referred to the importance of a lifelong commitment to understand the self, and how the self may or may not react in different situations. The lived life of a person is like a silk thread that is woven with other silk threads. The metaphor of the silk threads for community members who live together plays out to construct an elaborate tapestry. The final patterns of a single thread that contribute to the whole picture are dependent on the self-knowledge that an individual has access to as they pass through different stages or modes of understanding and knowledge and how this knowledge influences their activity and their responses to the environment and other community members. Kolb's theory of learning embraces the notion of an individual progressing through several life stages in 'human growth', during which an improvement occurs in the balance of the interests of the self and the interests of the community. This resonates with other humanist psychology such as Maslow's notion of self-actualization while also affirming Freire's (1995) plea for practices that are humanizing rather than dehumanizing. For example, using Eraut's modes of knowledge, it is potentially dehumanizing for individuals' lives to be spiritual, emotional and intellectual copies of others, and humanizing for them to be creative, original and authentic. However, the development of a unique individual is influenced by, and influences, their environment, communities and infrastructures. To understand this potentially heightens a person's awareness of how they influence the world around them, and how that world in turn shapes the way they influence the world. To add a further dimension to this, during postgraduate research a leader can explore how their own constructs were formed and through 'knowing thyself' future activity can be anticipated and changed. An intervention, can change the course of a person's life, by moving a person closer to a status of equity, and to working for social justice. Interestingly, the leaders that I spoke to said that their postgraduate research was an intervention in their life that changed their way of thinking and doing, and changed their personal growth on their learning journey. This is Senge's (1997) real learning that is fully actualized when engaged with as a group, so that a group's construing and re-construing may lead to more individuals 'knowing the self'. Referring back to the tapestry metaphor: people need people. This has the potential for people to begin to see how connected they are to each other, and may prompt civic responsibility and civic work within communities that is internally motivated. As Locke identified, a person who is internally motivated may achieve far more than one who is externally motivated.

Therefore, postgraduate research has the potential to encourage leaders to analyse their constructs and re-construe if they are to learn and if they are to develop as people and leaders. This process can be assisted if it takes place holistically. By this I mean that a leader's projected, and self-construct is analysed from the different perspective of their different roles for example a professional, a partner, a parent, a relative, a friend, a citizen, or the many other roles adopted by a leader in their lived life. A leader is a complex spiritual, emotional, intellectual, dynamic and creative human being. To further understand leadership a leader needs to build and test a sense of self.

Such a way of knowing will inform the leader about being critical of their own actions and facing their own truths that may be difficult to face. Further, such an approach may help them become more respectful and tolerant of others, as they realize that the whole truth of many situations remains hidden, and judging others without access to the whole truth is ill advised. This brings to light two very important questions: what is truth? And is it possible to know it has been found?

Search for truth

As stated in the first chapter, the foundation upon which knowledge was provided in the universities was a search for truth and Taysum (2006b) presents Barnett's (1999) suggestion that there were four core beliefs in the search for truth in the science and art of teaching, or pedagogy and pedagogic relations. The first was to be critical of the self, the second to be respectful of others, the third to be tolerant of opposing views and the fourth to be committed to the generation of new knowledge. Hall (1998) suggests that these core values underpinning pedagogy and pedagogic relations can be found in doctorates. The postgraduate researcher who approaches and engages with knowledge with these four values is presented with the opportunity to critique and challenge the common sense views, and the language that affirms them that may stand as barriers to social justice (Strain, 1998; Lubenow, 2002; Taysum, 2007a). Hall (1998) suggested that it is important to give individuals and communities the thinking tools to generate new knowledge, critique different conceptualizations of truth, and maintain respect for, and tolerance of human beings. Potentially, these core values will need to connect with the core values of the educational communities that the leaders serve. It is useful to have a framework to think through these different kinds of knowledge. Such a framework that aids thinking is called a conceptual framework, and it is like a coat hanger that keeps the shape of the clothes when they are not being worn. A conceptual framework, like a coat hanger for thoughts gives shape, and organizes a series of thoughts so that they are easier to understand. Therefore, epistemology is the knowledge of what is that may be organized into different series of thoughts or 'different epistemo- logical approaches'. Different epistemological approaches, or different ways of thinking help gain access to 'what is' or ontology. To be able to think about 'what is' there needs to be some object to think about. Equally, without knowledge or the capacity for thinking in different ways the concrete object or ontology could not be accessed, and arguably there would be no proof that it actually existed. Therefore, the way an individual thinks about the concrete, or 'the object' or 'what is' or 'ontology' may influence their relationship to and with the concrete object or 'what is' or 'ontology'. In turn the presence of the concrete object may influence the way an individual thinks about that object. For example, when one of our ancestors first picked up a rock and used it as a simple tool they may have begun to see other objects as potential simple tools. Using the environ- ment to improve quality of life in such a way transforms objects into other and more complex objects. Therefore, knowledge or epistemology influences the configuration of concrete objects, or the environment, or the structures or the ontology. As the concrete objects, structures, policies, legislation, environment or ontology transforms, knowledge or epistemology transforms. Both epistemo- logy and ontology influence each other in a stimulus-response-stimulus-response pattern. Such a relationship between the knowledge of 'what is' or epistemology and 'what is' or ontology might therefore be called iterative. What is import- ant to acknowledge here is that because every individual's way of thinking or epistemology is different and distinctive the way they access 'what is' or 'onto-logy' is also unique. This may not be a problem when thinking about objects such as 'rice' or 'wheat' or facts such as 'I am walking' or 'I am riding a bicycle' or 'I am driving a car' or 'I am on a train' or 'I am flying in an aeroplane'. However, accessing the ontology of complex situations is more problematic and poten-tially requires the gathering of the perceptions of many different people. This is important because one person's understanding of 'the truth' may be different to another person's understanding of 'the truth'. The roots of these different understandings, or indeed misunderstandings of ontology, may arguably go back to human beings' earliest or first ancestor, or 'the original form' or the source. Perhaps a human being's faith is an original source that is not predicated by the 'knowledge of the faith'. In this case faith is a committed belief that may be secular or non-secular. Therefore, faith needs to be carefully considered when engaging with epistemology and ontology. When seeking for the truth there are potentially as many versions of 'the truth' as there are human beings and this is highly complex. Potentially the best a human being can do is 'objectify' the information they have about ontology and make it clear that they are represent-ing a version of 'what is' or ontology when representing findings.

Postgraduate research provides opportunities for educational leaders to begin to think about their epistemological approach to their research, to con-sider their relationship with ontology and to consider the role of faith and values within the research. Therefore, consideration of different ways of thinking and doing at a particular time in a particular context can be done through postgradu-ate research that is systematic and trustworthy. The postgraduate research needs to address three or four key questions to meet particular aims and objectives. The researcher needs to critically reflect on the current knowledge by doing an in-depth and critical literature review drawing on credible sources (Oancea and Furlong, 2007). The review will need to compare and contrast different perspec-tives for each argument provided and these need to be carefully referenced, or justified so that the community member or consumer of the research can access the sources. The leader doing the research needs to be transparent about the sample or the participants in the research. The leader needs to be transparent about the systematic methods and data collection tools used to demonstrate trustworthiness, reliability and validity of the research (Oancea and Furlong,

2007; Levin, 2004; Pollard, 2008). The research also needs to be conducted within ethical frameworks (AERA, 2000; BERA, 2004; ESRC,2010). The perspectives or findings need to be represented and compared and contrasted with the current knowledge provided in the literature review. The evidence or new knowledge that is provided needs to be provided in a summary or a conclusion. The research needs to be disseminated particularly to the community that took part in the research. The new knowledge may be interpreted by and associated with the community which may move them towards understanding themselves, each other and their shared roles in taking responsibility for co-constructing a community of practice in new ways. In other words, the postgraduate research may shed light on how people might have copied and replicated solutions to old problems rather than interpreted and associated with new ways of thinking about 'what is' which may present new solutions to old problems. Thus postgraduate research leads to evidence informed leadership which develops new and shared understandings that may be a way of co-constructing and sustaining respect and tolerance of and for individuals within communities of practice. Educational leaders may start with small projects to build trust in communities and then move forwards step by step using the four core values of the university and systematic and trustworthy postgraduate research. To do this, postgraduate researchers need the thinking tools to begin to recognize the different systems of thinking or conceptual frameworks that give access to the concrete environment, structures, educational policies, legislation or 'ontology'. Lunt (2002) presents such a conceptual framework for different modes or ways of thinking. Taysum (2007b) rehearses that Lunt's (2002) conceptual framework begins with the notion that a mode of knowledge is the production of knowledge by argument or reasoning and is therefore a discursive production of knowledge. A discursive production of knowledge considers society's epistemological, institutional, cognitive and cultural dimensions (Delanty, 2001). Taysum (2007b) identifies that Lunt's (2002) conceptual framework is important for shedding light on four different discursive modes of knowledge or four different epistemological approaches found in postgraduate research. Lunt (2002) describes these as: 'Mode 1 Disciplinary knowledge, Mode 2 Technical rationality, Mode 3 Dispositional and transdisciplinary knowledge, Mode 4 Critical knowledge. Each mode will now be discussed. Disciplinary knowledge is about knowledge related to a particular field where examination and viva procedures are important for providing specified criteria to pass. In the main Lunt (2002) suggests these criteria are accepted by members of the academic community. Technical rationality, is where Lunt (2002) suggests practitioners: 'incorporate into their practice scientific knowledge that transcends the local and the particular'. Lunt (2002) describes dispositional and transdisciplinary knowledge as: non-predictable, non-deterministic, situation-specific and contextualized. Students are *taught* a number of ways of knowing and doing the research but no outcome is identified by the postgraduate programme. Critical knowledge focuses on developing an understanding of different ways of knowing and doing to enable learners to see things with fresh eyes (Lunt 2002).

Becoming critical is where dominant discourses are subverted (Barnett, 1997). Postgraduate researchers may dissent through the exposure to competing discourses, cultural models and institutional frameworks (Hall, 1998; Lunt, 2002; Ribbins and Gunter 2002; Gunter, 2005). Delanty (2001) calls this activity intellectual work. Through becoming critical, school leaders' may gain new insights into issues of social justice and equity (Taysum, 2006). This means that postgraduate researchers may begin to explore the gap between what they imagine they would like to do, and what is realistic for them to do (Bourdieu, 2000). If they can identify the gap, they can begin to critically reflect on how they can bridge the gap. From this experience, the postgraduate researchers, through evidence informed leadership, can invite their community members to learn how to become critically reflective so that they can identify gaps in their own lives and gaps in their communities. They can then begin to think about how they might become reflexive by thinking of ways in which bridges can be built to make their hopes for themselves and for their community become more of a reality. Such ways of knowing and doing may give access to knowledge that has been hidden about life and career trajectories and boundaries within and between the personal and professional lives of people. Arguably, this kind of intellectual work is emancipatory and humanizing and positions criticality as an important thinking tool (Freire, 1972).

Taysum (2007b) argues postgraduate research may also facilitate reflection (Schön, 1987). Moon (1999) suggests reflection occurs when assumptions are questioned that are the foundation of any other learning. Leitch and Day

(2001) present a tool kit to help organize three different types of reflection during the postgraduate research. First, the professional context is charted using mind-mapping processes. Second, autobiographical reflection on a critical incident is the focus of the group, or one to one discussion. Finally, through meta-reflection learners think about the process of reflection and recognize how they reflect and how they learn. In any of these forms of reflection, who the reflection is done with is of great import since it may cause individuals to change their self-perception which may in turn lead to a shift in identity, which can be risky (Thomson, 2006).

Fostering critical engagement with and reflection on current issues may lead to reflexivity. Reflexivity is where the new way of thinking impacts the professionals' change in praxis. I draw on Taysum's (2007b) understanding of Thomson's (2004) translation of Aristotle's lectures to define praxis as three elements: what an agent understands that includes a plan; what an agent chooses guided by right purpose, such as a desire for truth or respecting others; what an agent does to bring about change in the current state. Learning how to engage with such reflexivity has the potential to enable practitioners to work for change in their institutions (Fitzgerald and Gunter, 2005; Rayner *et al.*, 2002; Taysum, 2006a; 2006b). However, it is important to map the access to these thinking tools so that postgraduate researchers can make informed decisions about the construction of their evidence informed leadership.

The false dichotomy of theory and practice – important ways of thinking about practice

Postgraduate research connects theory and practice rigorously and this praxis is underpinned by research which informs the improvement of the learners' professional practice (Scott *et al.*, 2004). This is important because research is increasingly embedded within senior professional educationalists' environment(s) (Scott *et al.*, 2004). Taysum (2007b) argues that one of the aims of postgraduate research is therefore to develop individuals' research skills. This is affirmed by Scott *et al.* (2004), who state of the EdD: 'The overall aim of the degree is to produce people who are skilled consumers, evaluators, commissioners and producers of research' (p. 32). Theory and practice, or praxis enables the leader to begin to make sense of their activity in schools and to think through what is facilitating or presenting barriers to them actualizing educational policy for social justice. Such ways of thinking and doing may be generalizable or have leverage for other settings (Furlong and Oancea, 2005). This moves beyond the dichotomy of theory and practice to a recognition of a dynamic relationship between theory and practice. It is not possible to do something without thinking about it, and it is not possible to think without doing, and this relationship is called praxis (Grenfell *et al.*, 1998). It is arguably very important for a person to think about what they are doing. Indeed Arendt (1978) argues that from her research into war crimes from the Second World War, many atrocities were carried out with a total lack of thought of what was happening, and the consequences of what was happening. If a mistake is made, particularly in the case of war crimes, and no thought is given to it, then the same mistake will potentially be made again and again. To break out of a cycle such as this, learning about how others have handled such positions and/or mistakes, or in other words to access knowledge in the field is potentially helpful. This is different to copying solutions to problems from a manual which I referred to earlier. Rather, this is accessing knowledge, or accessing information that enables a leader to interpret and associate with action from their own and others' perspectives, while preventing re-inventing the wheel. However, as stated earlier this information needs to be trustworthy, reliable, systematic, and evidence informed to be robust which is why peer review is so important to gate keep the knowledge. Grenfell *et al.* (1998) argue it is important to:

> find a theory which is robust enough to be objective and generalizable, and yet accounts for individual, subjective thought and action. Moreover, the intention is to do so in a way that not only explains the logic of a range of social activities, including education, but also guides the practice of research into such activities. (p. 10)

I am, therefore, arguing that there is a false dichotomy between theory and practice because it is not possible to do something without some kind of thought even if that thought is on a very subconscious level such as the kind that keeps a heart beating. However, Woodhead (1998) is clear that theory is meaningless for teachers and they do not have the time to engage with thinking about what they do. If professional educationalists do not have the time and space to think about what they are doing, or think about what others have done, or are doing to improve education, then the same practice will be repeated. This same practice may be repeated in what has been labelled as a failing school. Such a reductionist approach is potentially dangerous. However, Woodhead makes an insightful observation that there is very little time for educational professionals to theorize issues such as social justice and emancipation through intellectual work. From my research I found many educational leaders supported Woodhead's view about the lack of time for busy professional educationalists to think about what they are doing. For example, Antonia, who has been a headteacher and is a consultant supports Woodhead's view and states: 'before I was a headteacher I was a deputy head for four years . . . Your reading is very limited. You don't have time to read all the research stuff'. This is validated by Joanne, a headteacher who is doing a doctorate, who states:

> I'm probably not a very good candidate to interview in that I've signed up for the [postgraduate course]. I've gone along to the lectures and done a quick couple of assignments. But really I haven't had the opportunity to put my heart and soul into it yet. I feel you know this first year I'm still treading water with regard to it and putting it aside until it needs doing, simply because of the nature of this job.

Joanne makes the point that her postgraduate research is put aside until it needs doing. On the other hand, Helen, a middle leader from England doing a doctorate, states: 'there's only my career and my university and that's about it. I'm so busy. Do you know what I mean?' There is no space in Helen's life for anything other than her career and postgraduate research. Jean, a deputy head at a secondary school doing postgraduate research also warns of the demands on the time of a busy professional educationalist. I asked her how she would answer if someone asked if they should engage with postgraduate research. Jean replied:

> I'd say go for it [doing postgraduate research] . . . Don't hesitate, don't

hesitate for a second. But the other issue is time. There is time to consider. Fortunately, I don't know whether I'm an insomniac or anything, I can work late at night and holiday time, I don't have family so my personal commitments aren't that huge. So holiday time I dedicate to writing and usually some part of the weekend, either Saturday or Sunday, I read . . . I would say to someone look at your time and what you can fit it in. But I think if you were someone who went to bed at 10 o'clock at night it might be difficult to fit everything in . . . but where there's a will there's a way. I know that I have certainly got far more out of it and in terms of what I've gained in experience and insights into meeting people and headteachers and colleagues and three outstanding educationalists it has been worth staying up until 2 or 3 o'clock in the morning.

Hannah, a headteacher and a doctor having engaged with postgraduate research in England, warns that studying for a doctorate as a part-time student is very challenging. Hannah states:

> that anyone who is full time, in full-time work particularly as a headteacher because I can't talk about it from any other perspective, and particularly if they've got a family, needs to think very very carefully about whether they should take this on because the time commitment is phenomenal. I've always sort of had the ability to exist on very very little sleep and if I hadn't been able to do that, I would have given it up only because it would have taken too much away from my family . . . I think people need to be aware that it is extremely demanding.

The learners' articulated experiences are validated by what the programme providers of postgraduate research have witnessed with regard to the educational leaders' learning journeys doing postgraduate research at doctoral level. An example of this is from Samuel, a doctoral programme provider from an English University, who states:

> I think the one thing they [learners doing postgraduate research at doctoral level] all have in common is that they find it very difficult to manage the demands of a job and home life and the demands of the doctorate and they've

all got that in common, and the ones who are most successful find a way of minimizing the demands of one or the other, the outside areas, home or job. The ones who do it successfully tend to find a way of doing that.

This is validated by a programme provider from an English university, who states that a doctor who graduated from the postgraduate doctoral programme:

said what she most valued about her research is the opportunity to focus on an area of education she cares passionately about in considerable depth because I have always felt strongly that research should be used to inform policy and practice. Undertaking doctoral research at the same time as working full time in a demanding job is not for the faint hearted but requires a single-mindedness and a commitment to the subject of your research.

This is validated by a professional researcher into EdDs, Anne, who states:

I think the interesting thing about EdDs is that many EdDs don't have many people from schools in them at all. I mean some of them are targeted explicitly at people, for example people from Higher Education. I think actually that for whatever reason school teachers may not have that much time to give.

The learners state that it is very difficult engaging with postgraduate research as part-time learners with leadership posts in schools and this is validated by the programme providers and professional researchers into the EdD. Leitch and Day (2001) suggest that time is a significant issue for practitioners who are part-time students, part-time family members and full-time workers. Joanne, Helen, and Jean state that they do not have family commitments that would pull them from their doctoral study. Hannah asserts that family considerations are extremely important and says she was able to engage with her postgraduate research at doctoral level for the EdD because she needs very little sleep. This is echoed by Jean, who states she works until 2 or 3 o'clock in the morning. Leitch and Day (2001) go on to state that it is recognized that finding the time to complete postgraduate research assignments is difficult. This connects with the splitting of the self into different roles and the blurring of boundaries between the professional and personal lives of a leader. This argument problematizes what is gained in a leader's learning journey. It does this, by highlighting what is lost in terms of sacrificing aspects of a lived life that may invoke feelings of guilt (Hargreaves, 1994), to enable learners to develop themselves as leaders holistically (Taysum, 2003).

Therefore, the evidence suggests Woodhead is right, there is little time for postgraduate research. The question remains, is he right that professional educationalists do not need time to think about their practice? Should the classroom be a location where lessons are copied from manuals, where teachers cannot think about how the learning and teaching relates to them and their students? Should learning and teaching be a balance between a 'national' prescribed curriculum and an authentic culturally relevant curriculum that recognizes teachers and students as spiritual, emotional, intellectual and physical human beings? At the core of this discourse is should teachers and students think critically and reflect upon what they are learning about and how it relates to their own communities and environments? This brings the argument back to the dichotomy between theory and practice, and the worth of theory.

It is important to think about who can consider and make judgements about what is to be learned. Mapping this discourse with regard to association with the curriculum and education policy may begin to throw light on the relationships of power that are dominant, subordinate or homologous (of equal power) in relation to individuals and the subgroups of their communities. Indeed, questions need to be asked about how dominant conceptualizations of the truth, or discourses, or particular sides in a debate may perpetuate the illusion of common sense. Further, how it has become common sense that teachers teach a prescribed curriculum needs examining critically. Such a debate is important when it is considered that the common sense may have come from people that Bourdieu (2004) describes as: 'the dominant figures who want continuity, identity, reproduction' (p. 106). The dominant figures are therefore able to shape the notion of common sense as a result of their position in the field and reproduce the unequal power share within the field. This is demonstrated by Schilling (2004) who argues that: 'the embodied actor is indelibly shaped by, but also an active reproducer of, society' (p. 474). This process continues until common

Activity			
Challenge	**Understanding meanings** *Conceptual:* challenging and developing understandings of ontology and epistemology. *Descriptive:* challenging and developing understandings of activity and actions.	**Understanding experiences** *Humanistic:* gathering and using experiences to improve practice. *Aesthetic:* appreciating and using the arts to enhance practice.	**Provision**
	Working for change *Critical:* to reveal and emancipate practitioners from injustice. *Axiological:* to clarify the values and value conflicts to support what is right.	**Delivering change** *Evaluative:* to measure the impact of role incumbents on outcomes. *Instrumental:* to provide strategies and tactics for organizational effectiveness.	
Actions			

Figure 4.1 Knowledge and knowing (Gunter 2005, p. 70).

sense is critiqued and reflected upon, which leads to reflexivity as identified previously. This new way of knowing has the potential to change an agents' practice and cause a possible shift in identity. This is arguably emancipatory if it frees agents up from invisible chains that prevented them from achieving what others can achieve because they have not been shackled with the invisible, but very real constraints. This may enable them to make more informed choices about how they relate to the ownership of their professional practice, and their identity as they move closer to becoming more autonomous. Educational professionals may then role model autonomous behaviour to their students who in turn may think more about what they do, how, why, where, when and with whom. This helps to address UNICEF's safety for risky behaviour. Approaching life choices with critical reflection may, therefore, enable leaders to make a more democratic contribution to their educational communities (Cribb and Gewirtz, 2003). Grenfell *et al.* (1998) suggest people have a *primary knowledge of their own situations* that they *have not reflected upon.* Underpinning this knowledge are all the previous experiences that have made them the people they are today. This is not just from their own life, but from generations before. Thinking about the primary knowledge as a thinking tool, may enable people to see things in new ways, and help unravel the origins of individuals' behaviour. When people begin to get to know themselves better in this way, they can begin to know the world differently. Therefore, the influence the world has on the individual shifts, and the influence the individual has on the world changes too. As stated previously, such transformation may lead to different career and life trajectories. Such a transformation depends on decisions being made that are based on reliable, and trustworthy evidence. It is therefore important to have thinking tools that enable those making decisions to be discerning about what can be counted as evidence, and what cannot.

Mapping different kinds of research so you know what you are doing – and you can defend it with evidence

Educational communities can acquire a false naturalness in the way that they understand their life choices. This is a false naturalness because their positions in society are not natural, rather positions have been constructed over generations where the language and the cultures constantly reaffirm and sustain inequalities whether this is intentional or not. The language and cultural inculcation may produce confident dispositions, or learned helplessness. Those who are confident may have been educated to be thus. However, those that demonstrate learned helplessness have arguably been part of a process of miseducation. Miseducation is therefore a problem. A pedagogic tool is required that can be used to examine this problem. A place to start may be educational policy, for example Every Child Matters and No Child Left Behind, that may reveal evidence of Dewey's 'education' or 'mis-education'. Therefore, the thinking tools of critical reflection are required that help leaders confront the taken for granted within educational communities. Klein and Sharpton (2009) identify some taken for granted assumptions that need addressing, the first being that only 34 per cent of black males graduate in Detroit, and in the nation's capital only 9 per cent of ninth-grade students complete college within five years. These kinds of issues need to be confronted if cash-poor black and Hispanic children are to begin to get the education that they deserve. The way the problem has been addressed to date, has not worked. Solutions are being copied, and they are not authentic, and they are not made through a democratic process that includes the people who are being affected by the solutions. These solutions may seek to provide a just education system and may be noble in intent, but they may unintentionally embed the miseducation that is occurring. It is not possible to make a judgement on this until different ways of examining the problem have been considered and the evidence systematically and rigorously scrutinized. Taysum (2007b) suggests a thinking tool to help postgraduate research programme providers and educational leaders doing postgraduate research to systematically and rigorously approach and engage with the evidence and how this might influence practice and have an impact in the field. The tool must provide ways of thinking about a problem found in practice in a consistent and reliable way. Taysum (2007b) suggests Gunter's (2005) typology of knowledge enables this (Figure 4.1).

This tool enables those engaging with postgraduate research to consider their research problem from different epistemological approaches (epistemology meaning the knowledge of what is), and to be transparent about the way in which they justify what they have selected and what they have de-selected with this important choice. There are five aspects to the enquiry that Gunter (2005) identifies as the positional which connects with life trajectories, and the way that people think about and experience transformations in their lives through learning experiences. The practical examines practice within the local and particular setting. The critical compares and contrasts the different arguments and potentially confronts common sense views and exposes where there may be social injustice. The illuminative inquiry considers policy, and all the cognitive, emotional and spiritual knowledge and skills a person may have. Finally, the technical enquiry examines scientific knowledge. There are four areas of approaches. First, delivering change where teachers passively deliver a prescribed curriculum, working for change, understanding experiences, and understanding meanings.

Gunter's four dimensions include understanding meanings, understanding experiences, working for change and delivering change. Gunter (2005) states that the typology of knowledge and knowing: 'has the potential to enable the field member to plan and undertake research in the field, and to critically evaluate other research' (p. 171). Gunter (2005) explains how the typology provides each of the four dimensions with five aspects to the inquiry. Firstly, the technical inquiry establishes the scientific knowledge surrounding the research and engages with the cognitive domain (Delanty, 2001). Secondly, the illuminative inquiry probes the meaning of the scientific knowledge. This process engages with institutional frameworks, cultural knowledge and the affective domain (Delanty, 2001). Thirdly, the critical locates the first two aspects within discourses and thus engages with issues of power, knowledge, hegemony and the cognitive and cultural constructs of society. Fourthly, the practical engages with practice in context. Finally, the positional engages with inquiry surrounding life and career trajectories (Bourdieu, 2000) and focuses on philosophy. Emancipation and transformations can come from these inquiries. Using Gunter's framework it is possible to see how viewing research through the dimensions of the typology of knowledge may prevent the privileging of one kind of knowing over another. Using Gunter's typology in such a way may be helpful for two reasons. First, it enables programme providers to assess the quality of the learning experience they are providing. This is made possible if the tool is used to interrogate the extent to which the learners have experienced each of the dimensions of the typology of knowledge during their learning journeys. Second, it provides learners with a working tool that may enable them to independently examine the quality dimensions of their own research. If leaders are not given the opportunity to access this kind of typology of knowledge on their learning journeys, then it may be left to chance as to whether they develop an understanding of the significance of different ways of knowing. This may mean that leaders start their postgraduate research within an existing epistemological approach for example the instrumental and/or evaluative domain and finish their post-graduate research still operating in the instrumental and/or evaluative domains without developing knowledge, skills or experience of other epistemological approaches. This would merely serve to embed the common sense view in a deterministic way and may not lead to emancipation and communicative action (Bourdieu, 2000). In such a scenario it is unlikely that policy as text would be critiqued, or interpreted in policy discourse (Ball, 2006). Rather, policy may potentially be transmitted through to schools. It is arguable that opening such an important window to knowing should not be left to chance. Perhaps, to move closer to social justice, it may be advantageous for learners to choose to select or de-select different ways of knowing and working as an informed choice. Programme providers, therefore, may find it beneficial to approach and engage with the postgraduate research curriculums using pedagogy and pedagogic relationships that introduce four elements. First, Barnett's four core beliefs, second, Lunt's four fold model, third, Eraut's (1994) interpretation of Broudy's (1964) four modes of knowledge and finally, Gunter's four dimensions represented in the typology of knowledge. It is important to note that there are alternative frameworks that might be drawn upon, for example Luckcock (2008, p. 378) presents Hodgkinsons' (1983) leadership archetypes and values para-digm, which gives another way of considering the different ways of approaching and constructing knowledge. What is important is that when the learner has grasped how these tools might help them develop their praxis, they are able to critique the tools themselves, and seek out others if they wish in a meaningful and worthwhile way. This resonates with Popper's argument represented by Fuller (2003) that the cost of gaining knowledge is that the knowledge will have a unique and arguably inaccessible affect on the knower in the very process of being gained, which is why being openly critical is a prime way of gaining insight into other knowers' unique relationship with that knowledge. This concurs with the argument that the main role of the university is to connect different conceptualisations of truth or discourses. This might enable the university to become a site of dissensus (Delanty, 2001), positioning the university as a place of public and moral debate that stands against the erosion of the public space (Delanty, 2001). Fostering critical engagement, reflection and reflexivity for evidence informed leadership in this way is realistic and may enable leaders to work for change in their educational communities (Fitzgerald and Gunter, 2005; Rayner *et al.*, 2002; Taysum, 2006a and 2006b), which might include enhancing community and civic responsibility.

Conclusions

To sum up, this chapter has examined how leaders might be developed to engage with evidence informed leadership through postgraduate research. Postgraduate research enables leaders to internalize research, policies or curriculums within ethical frameworks and make sense of them in their particular contexts with particular communities. This means that they will need to explore how the new ways of knowing and doing might connect with what is important to them, or their values. It will also call upon them to explore any emerging value conflicts and to support what is right. Such association takes courage to do and moves beyond copying and applying research findings, policies or curriculums without associating with the local and particular context. Associating with research findings, policies or curriculums is potentially implementing policies authentically and provides spaces for consulting with and working with the communities the leader serves. Thus postgraduate research may begin to facilitate the dispositions needed for civic work. Civic work of this nature might contribute to communities in educational settings moving towards better understanding themselves, each other and their role regarding civic responsibility. Issues of power will need to be considered when doing this kind of work, and it is important to understand how different people have different ways of understanding the world. An explanation of what is meant by epistemology and ontology was provided, and Lunt's conceptual framework of knowledge was presented to map different modes of knowledge. An argument that there is a false dichotomy between theory and practice was given because it is not possible to do something without thinking about it and to think about something without a concrete example of that action on which to base the thought on. This led to a discussion that there is little time to think about practice working within Ball's notion of 'performativity' and leaders' and postgraduate programme providers' perceptions were provided regarding how difficult it is to find time to do postgraduate research. At the core of this discourse was the notion of whether leaders and communities should think critically about what they are doing, or should they passively do what they are told. Arguably if an individual passively does what they are told, they are not engaging with civic work or taking civic responsibility. The case was made for evidence informed leadership that used authentic solutions to problems. Gunter's (2005) typology of knowledge; 'Knowledge and Knowing' (p. 70) was presented as a tool to help the knowledge producers, knowledge transformers and knowledge consumers think about their approach to research and the evidence systematically and rigorously. Using such a tool as a postgraduate researcher at a university has the potential to build leadership capability, capacity and to foster critical engagement, reflection and reflexivity for evidence informed leadership in the field. The next chapter explores the importance of critical analysis, reflection and reflexivity. Evidence is provided that sheds light on ways in which the academy supports the development of critical analysis with professional educationalists or groups of professional educationalists, to support 'peer-assisted learning' and evidence informed leadership.

References

American Educational Research Association (AERA) (2000), Ethical Standards of the American Educational Research Association [online]. Available at: www.aera.net/uploadedFiles/About_AERA/Ethical_Standards/EthicalStandards.pdf (accessed 24 May 2010).

Arendt, H. (1978), *The Life of the Mind*. New York: A Harvest Book Harcourt.

Barnett, R. (1997), *Higher Education: A critical business*. Buckingham: SRHE/OUP.

—— (1999), *Realizing the University in an Age of Supercomplexity*. Buckingham: Open University Press.

Beck, S. (2003), *Socrates Know Yourself*. Available at: http://www.san.beck.org.SOC1-KnowYourself.html (accessed 4 August 2003).

Biddle, B. and Saha, L. (2005), *The Untested Accusation*. USA: Scarecrow Education.

Bourdieu, P. (2000), *Pascalian Meditations*. Cambridge: Polity.

—— (2004), *The Field of Cultural Production*. Cambridge: Polity.

Bowden, R., Bourner, T. and Laing, S. (2002), Professional Doctorates in England and Australia: not a world of difference. *Higher Education Review*, 35 (1), 2–23.

British Educational Research Association (2004), Revised ethical guidelines [online]. Available at: http://www.bera.ac.uk/files/guidelines/ethical.pdf (accessed 24 May 2010).

Broudy, H., Smith, B. O. and Burnett, J. (1964), *Democracy and Education in American Secondary Education*. Chicago: Rand McNally.

Cribb, A. and Gewirtz, S. (2003), Towards a sociology of just practices: an analysis of plural conceptions of justice. In C. Vincent (ed.), *Social Justice Education and Identity*. London: RoutledgeFalmer.

Cohen, L., Manion, L. and Morrison, K. (2001), *Research Methods in Education*. London: Croom Helm.

Coleman, M. and Briggs, A. (2002), *Research Methods in Educational Leadership and Management*. London: Sage.

Crow, G. (2004), The National College for School Leadership Purpose, Power and Prospects. *Educational Leadership and Management*, 32 (3), 243–49.

Delanty, G. (2001), *Challenging Knowledge: The university in the knowledge society*. Buckingham: SRHE and Open University Press.

Dowding, K. (1996), *Power*. Buckingham: Open University Press.

Duffy, E. (1999), Leading the creative school. In H. Tomlinson, H. Gunter and P. Smith (eds), *Living Headship: Voices, values and vision*, pp. 105–13. London: PCP.

Duffy, J. (1999), *Harvesting Experience: Reaping the benefits of knowledge*. Kansas: ARMA International.

Economic and Social Research Council (ESRC) (2010), Framework for Research Ethics (FRE) [online]. Available at: www.esrc.ac.uk/esrcinfocentre/images/esrc_re_ethics_ frame_tcm6-11291.pdf (accessed 24 May 2010).

Eraut, M. (1994), *Developing Professional Knowledge and Competence*. Lewes: Falmer Press.

Fitzgerald, T. and Gunter, H. (2005), Trends in the administration and history of education: what counts? A reply to Rob Lowe. *Journal of Educational Administration and History*, 37 (2), 27–136.

Flessa, J. (2007), The trouble with the EdD. *Leadership and Policy in Schools*, 6, 197–208.

Freire, P. (1972), *Pedagogy of the Oppressed*. Harmondsworth: Penguin.

—— (1995), *Paulo Freire at the Institute*. London: University of London Institute of Education.

Fuller, S. (2003), *The Governance of Science*. Buckingham: Open University Press.

Furlong, J. and Oancea, A. (2005), *Assessing Quality in Applied and Practice-based Educational Research: A framework for discussion*. Available from: http://www.securewebmail.le.ac. uk/Exchange/ast11/Sent%20Items?RE:%20MIE%20article-5.EML/Furlong%20 and%20Oancea.pdf/C58EA28C-18C0-4a97-9AF2-036E93/Furlong%20and%20Oancea. pdf?attach=1 (accessed 3 April 2006).

Golde, C. M. (2006), Introduction: preparing stewards of the discipline. In M. C. Golde and G. E. Walker (eds) *Envisioning the Future of Doctoral Education Preparing Stewards of the Discipline*. Stanford: Jossey-Bass.

Golde, C. and Walker, G. (2006), *Envisioning the Future of Doctoral Education Preparing Stewards of the Discipline*. Stanford: Jossey-Bass.

Grenfell, M., James, D., Reay, D. and Robbins, D. (1998), *Bourdieu and Education: Acts of practical theory*. Oxon: Falmer Press.

Gunter, H. (2005), Conceptualising research in educational leadership. *Educational Management Administration and Leadership*, 33 (2), 165–80.

Hall, V. (1998), We are all adult educators now: the implications of Adult Learning Theory for the continuing professional development of educational leaders and managers. *ESRC Seminar Series: Redefining educational management*. Milton Keynes, England.

Hargreaves, A. (1994), *Changing Teachers Changing Times: Teachers' work and culture in the post-modern age*. New York: Teachers College Press.

Hodgkinson, C. (1983), *The Philosophy of Leadership*. Oxford: Basil Blackwell.

—— (1993), *Educational Leadership: The moral art.* Albany, NY: State University of New York Press.

Klein, J. and Sharpton, A. (2009), Charter Schools Can Close the Education Gap. It is not acceptable for minority students to be four grade levels behind. *Wall Street Journal*, 12 January [online]. Available at: http://online.wsj.com/article/SB123172121959472377. html (accessed 24 May 2010).

Kolb, D. (1984), *Experiential Learning: Experience as the Source of Learning and Development.* Englewood Cliffs, NJ: Prentice-Hall.

Leitch, R. and Day, C. (2001) Reflective processes in action: mapping personal and professional contexts for learning and change. *Journal of In-Service Education*, 27 (2), 237–59.

Levine, A. (2005), *Educating School Leaders.* New York: Education Schools Project.

Levin, B. (2004), Making research matter more. *Education Policy Analysis Archives*, 12 (56), 1–22.

Locke, J. (1909–14), *Some Thoughts Concerning Education*, (ed.) C. W. Eliot. The Harvard Classics, Vol. XXXVII, Part 1. New York, NY: P. F. Collier & Son.

Luckcock, T. (2008), Spiritual intelligence in leadership development: a practitioner inquiry into the ethical orientation of leadership styles in LPSH. *Educational Management, Administration and Leadership*, 36 (3), 373–91.

Lubenow, W. (2002), Making words flesh: changing roles of university learning and the professions in the 19th century. *Minerva*, 40 (3), 217–34.

Luke, A. (2006), Teaching after the market from commodity to cosmopolitan. In L. Weis, G. McCarthy and G. Dimitriadis (eds), *Ideology, Curriculum and the New Sociology of Education Revisiting the Work of Michael Apple*. London: Routledge.

Lunt, I. (2002), *Integrating Academic and Professional Knowledge: Constructing the practitioner-researcher.* Available from: http://www.qut.edu.au/dresa/CPE/ProfDocs/Papers/Scott_paper.doc (accessed 4 March 2003).

Maslow, A. (1954), *Motivation and Personality.* New York, NY: Harper & Row.

Moon, J. (1999), *Reflection in Learning and Professional Development.* London: Kogan Page.

Oancea, A. and Furlong, J. (2007), Expressions of excellence and the assessment of applied research. *Research Papers in Education*, 22 (2), 119–37.

Pollard, A. (ed.) (2008), *Quality and Capacity in UK Education Research.* Report of the first meeting of the UK's Strategic Forum for Research in Education, 16–17 October, Harrogate.

Quality Assurance Agency for Higher Education. (2007), The Framework for Higher Education Qualifications in England Wales and Northern Ireland. Available at: http://www. qaa.ac.uk/academicinfrastructure/FHEQ/EWNI/default.asp (accessed 24 May 2010).

Rayner, S., Gunter, H. M. and Powers, S. (2002), Professional development needs for leaders in special education. *Journal of In-Service Education*, 28 (1), 79–93.

Ribbins, P. and Gunter, H. (2002), Mapping leadership studies in education: towards a typology of knowledge domains. *Educational Management and Administration*, 30 (4), 359–86.

Riding, R. and Rayner, S. (2005), *Cognitive Styles and Learning Strategies: Understanding style differences in learning and behaviour.* London: David Fulton.

Robson, C. (2002), *Real World Research*, 2nd edn. Oxford: Blackwell Publishers.

Schilling, C. (2004), Physical capital and situated action: a new direction for corporeal sociology. *British Journal of Sociology of Education*, 25 (4), 473–87.

Schön, D. A. (1987), *Educating the Reflective Practitioner.* London: Jossey-Bass.

Schulman, L., Golde, C., Conklin, B. and Garabedian, K. (2006), Reclaiming education's doctorates: a critique and a proposal. *Educational Researcher*, 25, 25–32.

Scott, D., Brown, A., Lunt, I. and Thorne, L. (2004), *Professional Doctorates Integrating Professional and Academic Knowledge*. Berkshire: The Open University Press.

Senge, P. (1997) Through the eye of a needle. In R. Gibson (ed.), *Rethinking the Future: Business, principles, competition, control, leadership, markets and the world*. London: Nicholas Brearley.

Shields, C., Donmoyer, B., Mohan, E., Ghassan, I., Requa, D., Kose, B. and Taysum, A. (2009), A call for engagement: educational leaders as activists and public intellectuals. *American Educational Research Association Annual Conference*. San Diego, April.

Strain, M. (1998), Educational managers' knowledge: the quest for useful theory. In M. Strain, B. Dennison, J. Ouston and V. Hall, *Policy, Leadership and Professional Knowledge in Education*. London: Paul Chapman Publishing.

Taysum, A. (2003), In search of the holistic leader. *Management in Education*, 17 (5), 9–12.

—— (2006a), A *survey of the learning journeys of school leaders doing the Doctorate of Education in England*. Birmingham: University of Birmingham.

—— (2006b), The distinctiveness of the EdD within the university tradition. *Journal of Education Administration and History*, 38 (3), 323–34.

—— (2007a), The distinctiveness of the EdD in producing and transforming knowledge. *Journal of Education Administration and History*, 39 (3), 285–96.

—— (2007b), EdD research: does it have a future in developing educational leaders? *New Zealand Journal of Educational Leadership*, 22 (2), 22–36.

Thomson, J. (trans.) (2004), *Aristotle. The Nicomachean Ethics*. London: Penguin Books.

Thomson, P. (2006), Miners, diggers, ferals and showmen: school-community projects that affirm and unsettle identities and place. *British Journal of Sociology of Education*, 27 (1), 81–96.

Woodhead, C. (1998), Academia gone to seed. *New Statesman*, 26 March 1998. Available at: http://www.newstatesman.com/nsqpass.php3?num=10&QryTxt=Academia+gone=to=seed (accessed 15 April 2004).

Chapter 5

Confronting Taken-for-Granted Ways of Thinking and Doing that Limit Change

The fifth chapter examines how preparing and developing public sector leaders to use the thinking tool of critical analysis through postgraduate research, may be important. It is developed from a conference paper given at the American Educational Research Association as part of a British Educational Leadership, Management Administration and Leadershp Symposium (Taysum, 2008). The reason for this is that individuals may begin to question their 'gut reactions' and find them wanting. Stopping and thinking about assumptions or in other words *confronting* the ways of doing things that have been part of a person's life for a long time may be challenging, and uncomfortable. However, this process is important because it helps a leader get to know themselves better so that they can understand why they think and do things in the ways they do. This helps leaders to recognize alternative ways of thinking and doing that has the potential to reveal obstacles, thus enabling leaders to dislodge themselves from deterministic life paths or trajectories. Evidence provided by cases are offered, that shed light on ways in which the academy supports the development of critical analysis with professional educationalists or groups of professional educationalists, to support 'peer-assisted learning'. This may occur through organized postgraduate research or through In Service Education for Teachers (INSET).

Why becoming critical, analytical and reflective is important

Peters (1974) suggests teaching can be defined as both trying to, and succeeding in, imparting that which is worthwhile and moral to the learner(s). Here success may be evident by broad qualities such as accuracy, relevance, and the power to remain focused for marked periods of time. More particular virtues include valour, compassion, and grace (Peters, 1974). Hodgkinson (1991) suggests that teaching and learning about principles may begin to reveal the moral or value frameworks within which such qualities are located. However, study of this nature will inevitably involve recognizing both the light and the dark side of human behaviour. It frequently falls to educational leaders to make sense of the moral debates or discourses within society and to give the community members of their institutions the thinking tools required to enable them to recognize and understand the light and the dark side of the human condition (Hodgkinson, 1993). Therefore, educational leaders are caught up in societies' moral debates and dilemmas. The choices that they make, with regard to what is deemed worthwhile to be taught, are complex and of great significance to their communities. Pring (2005) argues that central to moral teaching is enabling learner(s) to make sense of the world, their environment and to give them the tools required to access further insights and experiences. If a teacher is able to achieve this, they potentially offer the learners the chance to develop as independent and autonomous individuals so that they might begin to make informed choices (Reay and Arnot, 2004). Confuscious suggests that acquiring the ability to recognize the changes within the environment and to gain the tools to be able to be flexible within that environment are also important.

Pedagogy is important here because, as Luke (2006) states, it is the art and science of teaching. Moreover, pedagogical relationships are those that are made together between teacher(s) and learner(s) (Peters, 1977). Peters (1977) continues that such relationships are best founded upon respect, but this does not exclude love. Rather love found in pedagogical relationships may be conceptualized as teacher–learner, rather than teacher–son/daughter. The learning is organized through the curriculum which is what is to be learned (Ross, 2000). This engages with different forms of knowledge.

Core to this book is critical analysis and reflection leading to reflexivity for evidence informed leadership. Taysum (2006a) suggests a pedagogical tool is required to help programme providers enable postgraduate researchers to map their use of criticality, reflection and reflexivity systematically. This is important if the researchers are to continue to engage with independent research after completing supervised postgraduate research. The pedagogical tool is called 'Learning to Critically Analyse and Reflect for Emancipation' or Learning to CARE (Figure 5.1).

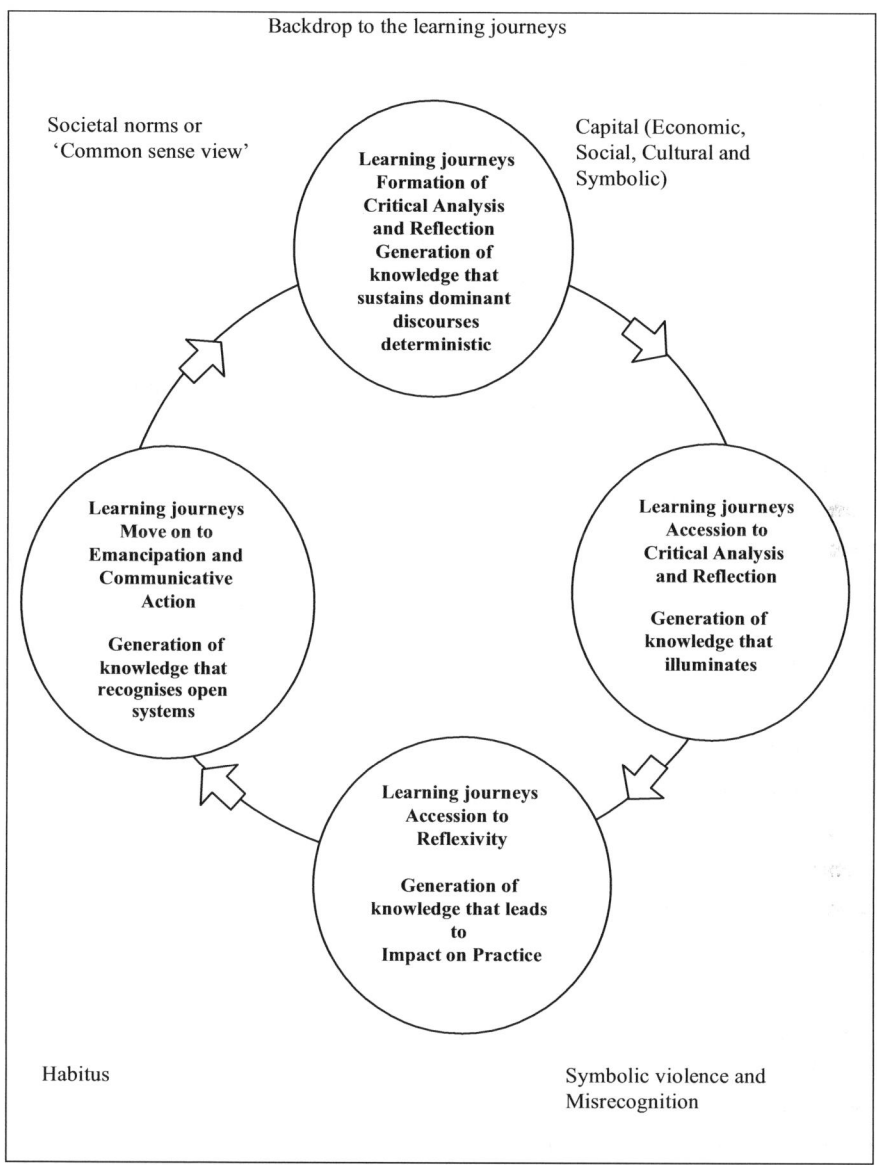

Figure 5.1 Learning to Critically Analyse and Reflect for Emancipation (CARE)
(Taysum, 2006a, p. 143). This figure shows the four-stage cycle of the
Learning to CARE pedagogical tool against a backdrop of important
elements as discussed in the main body of the text.

This pedagogical tool developed from research into Educational Doctorates and emerged as a way of understanding the evidence (Taysum, 2006a). Learning to CARE is a continuous cycle made up of four stages of the EdD learning journeys. First, the formation stage of Learning to CARE facilitates the development of skills in critical analysis and reflection. Here learners resist developing skills at the beginning of their learning journeys on the EdD, preferring to work with constructs that relied on their professional experience, their 'common sense' and habit (Bourdieu, 2000, 2004; Hall, 1998; Nash, 1999; Schilling, 2004). In other words the learners preferred to work with the capital they were comfortable with and their habitus was revealed through their practice (Bourdieu, 2000). Habitus is challenging to define because of Bourdieu's dislike of definitions, as labelling is potentially deterministic. What I mean by this is that the model of reality can become the reality of the model, which may be a barrier to systems that are open to social justice and social mobility. As stated earlier, Grenfell *et al.* (1998) suggest people have a *primary knowledge of their own situations* that they *have not reflected upon.* Underpinning this knowledge is the accrued experiences of antecedents from former hegemonies of generations and the agents who have shaped them. Therefore, habitus is revealed through practice and when used as a thinking tool, enables insights to be gained into individuals' primary knowledge and enables the accumulated experiences of antecedents to begin to be unravelled. The danger is to call habitus 'it', because it becomes defined and is potentially deterministic. It is important to understand that habitus moves beyond classification of the social world in terms of binaries and moves towards a structuralist constructivism (Taysum, 2006b) that is potentially emancipatory. Structuralist constructivism is where the ontological structures that I described in the previous chapter shape the way people build their knowledge of the world, or their epistemology and therefore the structures shape what they can and can not think and do. However, the relationship is iterative because what the people can and can not think and do in turn shapes the structures that shape their lives. The more powerful groups in societies can dominate the formation of the structures and can shape the common sense view that may be passively received by individuals. Therefore, particular hegemonies can shape identities through structuralist constructivism particularly if people do not develop the skills to be critically reflective and to engage reflexively in civic work. Therefore, if structuralist constructivism does not include critical reflection the generation of any new knowledge may ironically maintain the common sense view of the day and pedagogic work and activity (Bourdieu, 2000). Moreover, this may further embed misrecognition that continues to reproduce symbolic violence (Bourdieu, 1994, 2000, 2004) and presents barriers to social justice.

Misrecognition occurs when an agent's capital is not recognized, which results in one way of knowing being privileged over another. Bourdieu (2000) states when capital is misrecognized it becomes: 'a power or capital, that is a power, or capacity for (actual or potential) exploitation, and therefore recognized as legitimate' (p. 242). Misrecognition therefore prevents an agent from having equal access to opportunities that others with recognized capital have. Misrecognition relates to the ways social differences are embedded and perpetuated in the network of meanings and systems by not consciously acknowledging them. The common sense view, or legitimated, recognized way of knowing becomes dominant, and sustains a hold on the generating structures. This determines what is possible, or not possible to think or do by their axiological underpinnings, or values including value conflicts to support what is right (Gunter, 2005). In other words, by the values they attribute to activity (Grenfell *et al.*, 1998). Where there is misrecognition, therefore, there is social injustice and this is dangerous and does violence to agents that are misrecognized. This kind of violence is symbolic violence where dominant conceptualizations are imposed by one group, enabling it to rule another (Bourdieu, 2000). The kind of knowledge found at stage 1 of Learning to CARE synthesizes with Gunter's (2005) 'delivering change' (p. 170), with the evaluative and the instrumental being a preferred epistemological approach.

The second stage of the Learning to CARE pedagogical tool was accessing the thinking tools of critical analysis and reflection. This is where the learners were able to critically analyse and reflect on their learning journeys. This altered the way they perceived their practice, which was found to be illuminating. At this stage the learners shift to using this new way of knowing that illuminated their practice. Learners understood that their values, beliefs, behaviours and identities were shifting as a result of new insights they gained in the generation of new knowledge. This moved the leaders towards making decisions in complex settings that were informed by the evidence from their postgraduate research (Taysum, 2006a). Learners began to recognize how their capital (Bourdieu,

2000) had changed during their learning journeys and this was both uncomfortable and frustrating. Knowledge of this kind connects with Gunter's (2005, p. 170) 'understanding experiences' on Gunter's typology of knowledge, with the humanistic and aesthetic being the preferred epistemological approach.

Taysum (2006a) suggests the third stage was where the identities of the learners began to settle on their learning journeys and their critical analysis and reflection impacted upon practice in a process of reflexivity. This understanding became consolidated as learners moved beyond resisting how they had colluded in accepting and embedding a deterministic view of structuralist constructivism (Reay, 2004), to recognizing their role in reproducing and embedding social injustice (Bourdieu, 2000). This kind of knowledge affirms Gunter's (2005) 'understanding meanings' (p. 170) with the conceptual and the descriptive being the favoured epistemological approach.

The final stage is the 'move on' stage to emancipation. Here, leaders' reflexivity influences the school community through communicative action underpinned by the democratization of knowledge to generate knowledge that recognizes open systems (Bourdieu, 2000). The constructed evidence from postgraduate research informs leadership decisions and has the potential to remove barriers to social justice in the school community (Cribb and Gewirtz, 2003; Reay, 2003; Thomson, 2006; Gandin and Apple, 2002; Ball, 2006).

This kind of knowledge links to Gunter's (2005) 'working for change', with the critical and axiological being the preferred epistemological approach. Such enterprise has the potential to begin to realize policy agendas such as Every Child Matters, in England, and No Child Left Behind in the United States. This may be a way forward for leadership for the twenty-first century.

The four stages are part of an ongoing cycle because once the learner has completed supervised postgraduate research they may use the framework to map the application of the thinking tools important for evidence informed leadership in future independent research. Using 'The Learning to CARE framework' in this way, maps the intellectual tools of critical analysis, reflection and reflexivity leading to communicative action as leaders develop on their learning journeys. This gives opportunities for structural constructivism to remain an open system in the school community.

The four-stage framework is set against a backdrop of four dimensions.

First, considering the 'common sense view' of the learners enables the learning journeys to be contextualized by revealing what the learners perceived to be common sense at each stage of their learning journeys. This reveals the ways in which the learners move beyond embedding pedagogic work and activity in a deterministic approach to structuralist constructivism (Bourdieu, 2000; Delanty, 2001; Reay, 2004) to communicative action in open systems through a process of dissensus (Bourdieu, 2000). Second, habitus revealed through practice spotlights agents' individual career trajectories to be mapped out and enables the dualism between subjectivity and objectivity to be transcended (Bourdieu, 2000; Reay, 2004). This enables agency to be understood within spaces of limited choice that make access possible to open systems rather than determinism. Therefore, habitus enables structuralist constructivism to be revealed and understood through practice and for this reason, is arguably vital to the theorizing of postgraduate research and doctoral pedagogy in facilitating learning on postgraduate research programmes (Taysum and Gunter, 2008; Taysum, 2006a). Third, the four forms of capital described in Chapter 3 – economic, social, cultural and symbolic – provide a way of describing and understanding the learners' shift in identities as their capital changes over time on their learning journeys. Finally, symbolic violence and misrecognition are important aspects to the backdrop of the framework Learning to CARE. This is because the ways in which educational leaders misrecognized different ways of knowing in others and how they themselves may have been misrecognized is important to understanding the learning journeys on postgraduate research (Taysum and Gunter, 2008; Taysum, 2006a). This can be explained by considering how leaders of school communities embedded misrecognition by not recognizing the existence of misrecognition. This leads to symbolic violence (Bourdieu, 2000), which leads to the perpetuation of inequalities in society (ibid.). Such an analysis contextualizes the shift beyond the deterministic nature of the formation stage to emancipation and the recognition of open systems.

The role of postgraduate research in developing leaders to engage with evidence informed leadership

Taysum (2006a) argues that the programme providers and professional research-ers identified that the leaders on the EdD wanted to do postgraduate research and that study might improve their practice. Ann, a professional researcher into the EdD states:

> they [the learners] wanted to go in for some higher study, or wanted to have some professionally related higher study. They wanted to do some research that would be directly related to their professional practice that might enhance their professional practice. And they might also want to work in a cohort.

This agrees with Scott *et al.*(2004) who suggest that postgraduate research develops rigorous researchers and consumers of research, whilst respecting the knowledge and expertise of the educational professional. Further, Scott *et al.* suggest the leaders' postgraduate research connects theory and practice rigor-ously and this praxis informs the improvement of professional practice. Ann's findings also agree with the QAA (2008) that is required at doctoral level, that the leaders who have done postgraduate research will have the ability to make informed judgements on complex issues in their professional practice and will tackle and solve problems. These findings are validated by Jane, a postgraduate research programme provider for the doctorate, from an English university with the pseudonym Atlanticar University. Jane states:

> first and foremost we [the programme providers] are researchers and our students know what they've come into, we make it very clear in all our publicity material that they are coming to do a research degree. They're in no doubt about it.

Philip, an EdD programme provider in a university in the United States, with the pseudonym Colorado River University, articulates that a careful approach to research is very important:

Well I suppose the simplest definition of research would just be to think about something carefully, and careful thought would be the opposite of just random shoot from the hip activities. So that is what we are trying to do, and not just in education but in human endeavours generally, is to provide a more thoughtful, careful approach, to see if we can determine what our assumptions are, to open them to examination, to use data, observations to better understand what it is that we are doing, and to open up debate over whether or not something is the best approach. So that instead of taking things as a matter of doctrine or a matter of faith we are interested in examining things and using a scientific method, and using philosophical methods to better understand the world in which we are living . . . We could talk about values. Let us say, if we would value a democratic approach, I think that research would have a role to play in terms of helping us to define more carefully what we would mean by a democratic approach and where we would want it to happen and how we would develop democratic values, what leads to them, what doesn't lead to them. So you start with values that are important and perhaps a faith that certain kinds of things are important but that it is balanced with research for understanding.

Moreover, the findings from the programme providers identified that postgraduate research engaged with intellectual work. Elizabeth, a programme provider from Pacificar University, states:

I knew the importance of masters work both for myself and my own experience and also for practitioners that I had worked with both in [name of place] and [name of place] and that people valued that kind of work. And working on the EdD and working with practitioners on the EdD would allow me to continue to make a contribution to practitioner development. Not just through the taught element but through the emphasis on research. I have a very strong commitment in my work to the importance of intellectual work. That professionality is not technical, it is not just about what we do and how we do it. And it is not just about pragmatism of 'what on Earth do I do now on a Monday morning when this problem has come to my door'. It is actually a very strongly philosophical, intellectual job where you have got to have some distance from practice in order to think through tough issues around how we want to work with children and work with our colleagues and make a contribution to democratic development and therefore the EdD facilitates that. It gives people space to do it, it gives them the position to do it and it's longitudinal. It is not quick and dirty like – you know – here we are go on a course, learn how to do this – put it into action Tuesday morning. That kind of activity is important but it is actually longitudinal study that allows people to be challenged and to challenge and I don't think that we will get the profession that we need and children and adults deserve, without it.

Moreover, Theresa, a dean in a university in the United States with the pseudonym Green River, who oversees doctoral programmes at the university states that postgraduate research gives learners the chance to do research so that they can make decisions that are evidence-informed which will enable them to trust themselves. Theresa states:

[E]ducation is such an applied field and yet a field that is permeated by theory and it is why ultimately for me I don't think I see the need for a great distinction between an EdD or a PhD. Because I think that the theory's important and the learning to do the research primarily for those people who will never do research on-goingly so that they really do careful work in working through problem solving and become more effective consumers of others research and Lord knows there is enough bad research that is out there, that being able to have some ability to discriminate between research that really tells you something about what makes a difference in students' learning in given contexts, for example, versus something that is just some amazing con, sort of distortion of statistics or a findings section, a discussion section that doesn't really relate exactly to what the findings found. And being able to make that distinction so that when one is looking for resources to help make good decisions that one can discriminate what is really telling you something that is worthwhile and what is not and again in education the problems are almost all ill defined there is so much policy that is not grounded in thoughtful problem solving that in my opinion that would have a research approach to it even if it wasn't the lengthy thing of the dissertation. So I'm just thinking about a conversation

I had yesterday with a representative from the [name of school] public school district and the district had identified eight competences that they determined were essential to being an effective teacher. And this individual who has a wonderful educator, administrative but also scholarly frame of mind and has worked with them and has been educating future teachers for six years now, says, and of course we didn't have it right. And I said, why didn't you? And he said, because we have been fostering these characteristics of teachers but we haven't been looking at the association of these characteristics to their students' learning . . . So the step is to start thinking through what does that mean? It is that kind of enquiring mind, you know scholarly enquiring mind that I would hope for in a doctorally prepared administrator or policy researcher or faculty member . . . when I was teaching I would occasionally include an article by someone considered an expert but where the methodology or the conclusions or whatever were not all that strong, and I would ask the students to analyse the article with me, and try to encourage them to ask their own questions of what they had read, and then say look, you know you are as smart as, if not smarter than, you have come to conclusions that enable you to see that this was not necessarily a strong piece of research, therefore don't trust everything that you read. Trust yourself, you can learn from the stuff . . . but just learning that confidence is tremendous.

Leaders doing postgraduate research agree with the postgraduate research programme providers that their research was important for their development. Matthew a headteacher of a primary school at phase 2 of the EdD programme from Atlanticar University, a pseudonym for a university in England, states:

Well I think it's given me license to be more critical of anyone in the LEA or DfES or whoever, to take most things with a proverbial pinch of salt and to . . . I suppose it's given us, given me and the senior management team extra power if you like, to make decisions if we think they're right even if they might not agree or coincide with LEA ones or national ones and not to be afraid to be different if you think it's the right way to go, not for the sake of it but to look for creative solutions basically which don't necessarily correspond with current solutions.

Charlotte, a deputy headteacher of a secondary school in England, is at phase 3 from Pacific University, a pseudonym for a university in England, and states:

> It's [the EdD] relevant, it's totally relevant to what I do. And to my aspirations. So we are talking about a course that is targeted at someone like me who is a leader but who wants to take on different leadership roles within education. So it was targeted at me. It was dealing with things that I knew so there was a model of middle management and at the time I felt I was middle management. But at the time it was also giving me opportunities to interview senior management so you were beginning to do all those things that aid your fulfilment of your aspirations. And whatever metaphor you might want to use in terms of going up a ladder or rising in the organization or whatever, whatever you want to see that as it was giving me the things like networking because I was talking to headteachers for my own research, more particularly it was giving me much more. So it was giving me the breadth, a broader insight into education. And it was enabling me to discuss the very thing that I was wanting to be good at. So it was interesting to be able to hear what a range of headteachers say about leading and managing in schools. So some of the modules in particular pinpointed at what I was interested in. But then of course having the choice of my research, that could be entirely what I was interested in because that is a free choice.

These findings resonate with the argument presented by Scott *et al.* (2004) that postgraduate-research doctoral study on the EdD develops rigorous researchers and consumers of research who construct evidence-based practice. This becomes evidence informed leadership when the leaders use the evidence to inform decisions within their communities of practice. Moreover, these findings conform to the QAA published criteria of doctoral level qualifications. Here postgraduate researchers doing doctorates design and implement projects to generate new knowledge. This knowledge is used for Evidence Informed Leadership in complex educational settings.

The evidence agrees with Flessa (2007) who rehearses educational leaders are well served by EdD study and the intellectual work it demands. Moreover, the evidence agrees with Eraut (1994) that postgraduate research enabled the educational leaders to better associate with their current and future professional practice. The findings also resonate with Middleton (2007), who argues that doctoral study as a particular form of postgraduate research presents opportunities for learners to gain new insights from their intellectual work.

Accessing thinking tools for undertaking postgraduate research

I asked the school leaders how they were handling becoming critical, critiquing issues of power and constructing evidence to inform their leadership. The responses I received were varied. Joanne a headteacher of a primary school and now a deputy director of Children's Services at phase 1 from Pacificar University stated: 'In what way? I don't understand the question . . . I don't know the answer to that. I don't know. Can I say I don't know?' This is a very different response to that of Helen, a learner at phase 2 of the EdD programme at Pacificar University, England. Helen states:

> Before I did the EdD course I accepted that whatever was written was true and I still have this . . . a respect for . . . it's almost a respect for people and I still think well if they've said it, it must be right and one of the hardest things I find is to say well they said that, but in actual fact it's not right because I think, and I find that quite difficult because I still . . . somebody's written it, somebody's put it in the book, therefore they must know what they're talking about and it must be right. But now I'm questioning that. I am questioning it, but still find it hard.

Dasha, a postgraduate researcher doing a master's degree at a Russian university with the pseudonym Mockba River University, argues that being critical and comparing and contrasting different views from the field enabled her to find gaps in her own thinking. Dasha states:

> It gave me some other critical opinions which actually showed some points in my work which still needed some extra work.

Jean, a deputy headteacher of a secondary school at phase 3 from Pacificar University, England, states:

> I think in a secondary school in particular and perhaps in a leadership role, there is a tendency to get things done de, de, de, de, de, de, de, there is a pressure to get things done. I think it is so important to step back and start asking those questions well why?

Charlotte, a deputy headteacher at a secondary school at phase 3 from Pacificar University, England, states:

> And there is something I can directly attribute to the EdD there as well and that is the resistant headteacher, Gerald Grace, who has looked at different types of headteachers and the headteacher I researched for that very first module, I identified as being a resistor and I'd always seen a resistor as being, resistance I had always seen as being negative, because I had always thought that you should not resist progress and change and that you should move forward and develop. So of course it's not is it? Resisting is not doing things that you don't want to do that you don't think are right. So that research that I did there totally changed my view of a single word – resistance – and I realized that was something I valued being able to sort out what was the right thing to do. And I am still astonished at how few people at some meetings that I go to at the same sort of level as me, they would be deputy heads and assistant heads in secondary schools locally and they demonstrate regularly their own sense of disempowerment in the face of government initiatives, LEA initiatives.

Lawrence, a full-time PhD student at a university in the United States between phase 2 and phase 3, articulates that the PhD is enabling him to become more aware of issues of social justice and how to respond to them. Moreover, he wants to act as a bridge between the academy and the classroom by being a professor and a principal or superintendent. Lawrence articulates how he understood his learning journey to becoming more critical:

> Let me see, when I was teaching in the school with predominantly Latino

students and Latino teachers the administration was also Latino and so when the teachers and the administrators or principals would talk, I would say I think I have this suggestion and I would raise my hand they would recognize it, but they would never really consider it, it wasn't anything that had any value to it. I always thought why? I had a masters degree, just because I was an employee I had a say so, but unless in their eyes I was one of them you are not really going to have a say so. They would not really attend to teachers . . . the principal was doing what ever he wanted to, and we thought if you are going to ask us what we think and then at the end of the day you are going to do what you want, that is frustrating. Then somehow the way that it was, it would sort of condition us and got into the mind of the teachers because the teachers would do that to the students and the teachers would say we are going to do this project and we are going to do it this way, and the students would say wait a minute, woe, I want to be able to do it this way and this way, and this way and the teachers would say, 'no, no, no, no, no', so you really had this kind of snowball effect that just kept making itself bigger and bigger and bigger because of the fact that it trickles down from the principal who doesn't really consider the teacher, who doesn't have any voice, and then the teacher who doesn't see the student as having any voice either. So again it is the power structures at play and helping my colleagues see that is very difficult work. A lot of my colleagues in the classroom tell me that I am crazy and they say they don't do that, and I say do you think there is anyone who does that, but they don't want to see it or they don't think they are capable of doing it, but on some level subconsciously some people still do it.

Alison: When do you think you began to recognize that this was happening?

Lawrence: You know it wasn't until I got into the PhD programme. I was a teacher I taught the way I was taught and that's not the smartest thing to do, but when I came to the university and was exposed to different philosophies schemologies, and learned what an ontology was I really started to put things into perspective. I thought you know, this is true, I have done this and I feel bad. I have somehow been that person that the literature says, or at least have had feelings like that and it is not until I got into the programme that I was opening my eyes to the inequities that I was perpetuating, not consciously but still they were I think inequities that I was perpetuating because I didn't know, and half the problem is knowing right?

Alison: Has that been an easy path to follow?

Lawrence: No, it is not easy at all.

Alison: Can you tell me a bit more about that?

Lawrence: There is one particular philosophy, 'critical race theory', that tends to look at how certain groups are marginalized and not given a voice. I really felt that when I worked at a school that was practically 100 per cent Latino. We really did not do enough, I guess. We really didn't discuss or have those conversations of why certain students were not passing their classes or why certain students were not coming to school, and certain teachers just thought that was the nature of those students. I said I never really voiced my concern about that, but I think a lot of times there are a lot of misconceptions that people make because and I speak of my experience where the students were Latino . . . we are perpetuating the system, that allowed them to give up because we don't put the system in their favour we push them out of school we don't engage them with anything of their interest, we don't do any of that. You are familiar with the standardized testing well schools here in [name of school] are plagued with this test. They must pass because teachers' jobs are at stake and so teachers are teaching this one way and if you don't learn this one way then you are out and for a student who is an immigrant from Mexico, he or she is going to need a lot more than a test to be productive in school. And so I really thought about how people when they don't know these things that I have been learning during the [PhD] programme can really have detrimental effects on the students. I saw all the time, that the students (thought oh my teacher doesn't care about me) [*sic*], but the teacher probably did care, but the system didn't really give them that avenue to care. How could they, there is a test that they must pass in order to keep working and employed and everything is at the expense of the student. Again, that power that comes from above, above, above, above that trickles down, and the only ones left at the bottom are what we are in this business for.

Alison: Is the language of instruction an issue with these students?

Lawrence: I would say, yes we don't do enough of incorporating or
valuing the language the student brings with them, for example in
[name of school] that I worked at, the students spoke Spanish that was
their first language for example. So for an English teacher the fact that
they could not read Shakespeare or Chaucer and *The Canterbury Tales*
was the reason at least as far as the curriculum why they should fail,
they couldn't read it. But I think as a teacher who recognized them and
really tried to take their language and let them read stories in their own
language I think it was responding to their culture. I wasn't perpetuating
the inequity because a lot of times it is the instruction because we are
(using) this book (from the) [*sic*] curriculum here you go and you teach
this and there you go off and teach it and the students don't have any
say so of what they want to learn and how they want to learn it, and what
language it is in. In the United States after elementary the instruction if
I am not mistaken has to be in English. I think in elementary levels the
instruction can be in Spanish but I think as far as high school goes here,
at least where I was at, the instruction needed to be in English, all text
books needed to be in English. Of course that is a problem and some
folks don't really consider that an issue and so we make light of that so it
continues happening unfortunately . . . but for those of us who recognize
the inequities that occur in the classroom we can actually implement
other stories and ask the students to speak in their own language and
still they are learning. Of course language is important but making their
own language valid as well is part of the solution to helping them being
successful . . . I think that the PhD has influenced me as being a leader in
the sense that it has made me more confident, that is for sure. It has given
me the voice, the energy, the knowledge, I want to say to fight for what
I believe in, but I don't want to say fight, that is such a bad connotation
. . . To really make a change, make revolution in education. I honestly
think that the PhD can get me what I need to. My heart is in being a
professor. My hopes and dreams are to be a joined up professor one
day, but I also would like to still continue practically in the capacity of a
principal or superintendent so that I can merge and help the professors

at the university bring down that stuff they write in journals like AERA and UCEA and really make it accessible to educators with relative issues that is really going to help them make a difference. I am not saying that the educator won't understand the philosophy part or anything but it just needs to be more accessible to them written in a journal that they would read. Again I think the PhD has given me confidence that I can do it, I can make a change.

Lawrence's desire to bridge the academy and the classroom ties in very closely with Delanty (2001), democratization of knowledge where the university acts as a site where discourses can be compared and contrasted. This approach agrees with Irena, who is engaging with postgraduate research at masters level in a Russian university with the pseudonym Mockba River University. Irena articulated that there were four ways in which being critical during her postgraduate research had helped her. Irena states:

When we do research, we are taught and asked to present different points of view on our topic. It shapes the research so well, when you have some points to argue and prove with your evidence. One of the recent works I did was for my speciality diploma. The topic was the methodology of teaching reading in English with the use of project work method in elementary school. There was a position of one of the authors that project method is not to be used in elementary school. Another one was that history and geography are not to be included as topics for texts in English, because courses of history and geography begin only in middle school. I argued both positions by bringing evidence of the educational experiment we did, and presenting works of other authors and researchers. My research showed that children of an elementary school age are perfectly able to cope with projects when guided by a teacher and taught how to do it. Also they expressed a great interest in history and geography of the English-speaking countries and were able to get sense out of the texts . . . So by presenting this outcome in argument with another point of view I've shaped my research and proved it useful. But also personally I think when you work with a different position, sometimes it's more logical then your own and finally you could change your idea to the opposite one if you're reassured and have found the evidence. Although, I haven't experienced it yet in my work.

Hannah, a headteacher of a primary school at phase 4 from Pacificar University, England, said doing postgraduate research had enabled her to critique structures that structure agency and this had given her insights into issues of power. This had affirmed her belief that members of the school community can be given realistic chances to change their life trajectories that would not be part of a common sense view. Hannah cites the following example to illustrate this:

I'm absolutely committed to professional development for everybody, so we had a mom who worked in the kitchen at my last school who was just . . . so intelligent and witty . . . and she came to me and asked if she could do some work in the classroom and in those particular days to support children with special needs you didn't need any particular qualifications. I mean of all the people to put with two Down's Syndrome children, somebody with experience in the kitchen and nothing else and you'd say, oh gosh you know and the most needy children, but she was brilliant, and she really confirmed that that was the right thing to do, because she then got the bug that I'd got and had to go to college in the evenings and was constantly coming to me and you know, how do I get to do this and how do I get to do that and I was constantly saying look you've done this now, come on what's next. She's now a teacher and not just a teacher, a superb teacher. So being committed to getting people to achieve the things that perhaps they hadn't had the opportunity to achieve. But also to making sure that they gained access to power. Okay it's about powering her life to actually maximize all the abilities that she had but it's also about power in school because not only did she become a teacher, she had a leadership role and even before she was qualified as a teacher when she was working as a classroom assistant, I made sure that the area she could lead, she was leading. So she was developing as a leader before she was even qualified as a teacher and really trying to make sure that through professional development people have the opportunity to develop that leadership and that yes it is a shared leadership. I have to say that I'm very much of the opinion that the most effective way in school is to have a shared vision.

Henry, a headteacher of a secondary school, consultant and doctoral student at phase 4 from Indianar University, a pseudonym for a university in England, said doing postgraduate research and constructing evidence-based practice was very important to his development as a leader. He also said this work was hard and: 'gave me a headache'. Henry goes on to state:

It [critical analysis] was helpful and I think it was helpful in my job as well because I became more rigorous about how I put things down on paper, certainly as a result of it. I can't sort of think of any examples, but you just had to be so careful about how you put things and not to put any kind of innuendo or personal view into something unless it was backed up by evidence. So you had to have some evidence in order to support any statements and I think all too often as heads we make well probably teachers as well make a lot of statements which if they really were self-critical they weren't sufficiently backed up by evidence. I mean as teachers we talk such a lot and I think that 80 per cent of it is not backed up by evidence. So I learned really to, in my work to be more structured about how I was presenting material and I would say the reason for it, the evidence base for it. So having a challenging mind and evidence to support a change is a critical part of school improvement. Now it can be that if you haven't got that kind of challenging instinct you make sort of assumptions about the way you are doing things, that they are the only or the best way of doing things and in particular the major study that I did was about – in simple terms – it was looking at another school or part of it was looking at another school that was in a similar context to my own school and recognising that the progress of the children was better in that school than it was in mine. And saying what is it that is going on in that school that I'm not doing, or that my school is not doing and is that likely to bring about improvements in my school. Now that is a very fundamental and serious question about the way you are doing the job and actually saying let me find someone who is doing their job better and ask the question. You know, could I be doing my job better? And so without going through that process, there is a danger that you can think that you are doing your job pretty well and the reason that the other school is doing better is just kind of by chance or because they have better staff. You know, you can always make excuses for why other people or other staff are doing better than yourself.

The evidence reveals that critical analysis of common sense assumptions connects with subverting dominant discourses (Barnett, 1997, cited in Delanty, 2001; Hall, 1998; Lunt, 2002). The evidence suggests that learners at phase 1 of their doctoral studies did not understand what critical analysis of issues surrounding power was. Learners at phase 2 of their doctoral studies understood what critical analysis of issues surrounding power was, but found it difficult to do because the habit of accepting the common sense view had been embedded in their constructs. Learners at phase 3 of their doctoral studies perceived critical analysis of issues surrounding power as significant and emancipatory. A critical approach gave a different way of knowing, a resistance to a dominant discourse which had previously been perceived as a negative activity. Critical analysis was therefore reported to be an emancipator when founded on empirical evidence and had a direct impact on leadership. Learners at phase 4 of their doctoral studies all reported that critical analysis had been an emancipator and that this approach had impacted upon their practice through reflexivity as leaders engaged with communicative action within their communities. (Bourdieu, 2000). By this I mean the leaders were careful to base judgements that had an influence on the lives of their community members on evidence while giving them the opportunity for their subjective expectations to meet their objective chances. Such activity arguably underpins Evidence Informed Leadership.

The one exception to this was Matthew, a headteacher of a primary school at phase 2 from Atlanticar University, England. Matthew reported that he was critically analysing the interplay between structure and agency and that his practice was changing as a result. However, Matthew revealed in the interview that he had engaged in learning programmes that explored sociology prior to doing the EdD. He stated this prior learning had made him 'pretty aware of those sorts of issues and the socio dimension shall we say'. His self-perception may go some way to explaining why Matthew was engaging with evidence informed leadership when he was at phase 2, a relatively early phase of his doctorate.

All the leaders reflected upon their learning journeys on the EdD during the interviews. Each discussed how their reflection had enabled them to reframe their praxis in different ways (Taysum, 2006b). Jean, a deputy headteacher of a secondary school at phase 3 from Pacificar University, England, states: 'It's made me more reflective. It's made me appreciate how lucky I am. And it has made me appreciate that I'm at the right school'. Antonia, a headteacher of a secondary school and consultant at phase 1 from Atlanticar University, states:

[I]t's [the EdD] given me a better understanding of the dynamics of organiza-tions and you know, before becoming a head, while I understood that, I hadn't really researched it or thought deeply enough about it. Now if I go back in the role I go back with a clearer understanding of what it means as far as schools are concerned and you know, an understanding of why people behave the way they do and the sorts of things that you want to do in order to get what you want, to achieve what you want and I do think culture . . . is very complex and hard to change.

Helen, a headteacher of a secondary school who has taken two secondary schools out of special measures from Pacificar University at phase 2, demonstrates that reflection can be illuminating and reveals her career trajectory was limited by not passing the eleven plus:

I didn't pass [the eleven plus] to go to the grammar school. I went to the secondary modern school which was an all girls school and we, although I was in the top stream for most things, because it was a secondary modern school, it was very much you were expected to do a practical thing. So at the end of your time in your school, you'd go out and you'd be a nurse or you'd go out and work in an office. There were no 'O' levels or a higher . . . sort of thing open to you.

Helen states that she: 'wanted to work with people and help people to learn', which is interesting because she sought help from people to learn and found it when access to doctoral work became a reality. Therefore, her subjective expectations and the objective chances (Bourdieu, 2000) met in the offer of an EdD. Previous to this, Helen's subjective expectations had been irrelevant since the objective chances were not available and she had been excluded from postgraduate research. The evidence presents that the application of the reflection work did challenge the leaders' perception of the self, both professionally and personally (Leitch and Day, 2001) and as such led to a shift in identity (Thomson, 2006). This is developed further when the critical analysis and the reflection leads to reflexivity.

Learners articulated that their postgraduate research had facilitated them to becoming more critical, and reflective. This they argued had underpinned their reflexivity. These leaders had experienced a shift in identity. An example is provided by Hannah, a headteacher from a primary school in England, a learner and at phase 4 of the EdD. Hannah states that she found her learning journey enabled her to recognize how she was seeking permission to be doing a doctorate. Hannah stated:

> I think that [the EdD was] really helpful . . . because you know, there were people from south of 'place', from east and west and people from such different areas and all feeding off each other and quite challenging people who were much more confident than I was because I suppose in the same way that I was sort of seeking permission to be the headteacher because I was a woman, I was also sort of needing permission to be doing a doctorate.

The evidence reveals how life and career trajectories were reframed and individuals were able to make more informed choices about their futures through evidence informed leadership. These leaders have a strong sense of recognition of symbolic violence, pedagogic work and activity (Bourdieu, 2000). The knowledge they generated illuminated barriers to social justice. They were able to connect this new way of knowing and doing to their practice. The new knowledge that these learners generated as a result of their intellectual work on their learning journeys enabled them to work for change both personally and in their professional practice. They achieved this by presenting others with windows of opportunity to understand how they might make more informed choices.

Mapping the learning journeys of the school leaders on the Learning to CARE pedagogical tool

I now read the data through the Learning to CARE pedagogical tool to map the leaders' use of the thinking tools critical analysis, reflection and reflexivity for evidence informed leadership. Learning to CARE is a continuous cycle made up of four stages of the learning journeys. First, the formation stage of Learning to CARE facilitates the development of skills in critical analysis and reflection. The empirical evidence demonstrated that learners resisted developing these skills at the beginning of their learning journeys on the EdD. They had more confidence working with constructs that relied on their professional experience, their 'common sense' and habit (Bourdieu, 2000, 2004, Hall, 1998; Nash, 1999; Schilling, 2004). In other words the learners preferred to work with the capital (Bourdieu, 2000) they were comfortable with and their habitus was revealed through their practice. The empirical evidence demonstrated that this approach led to the generation of knowledge but that this new knowledge maintained the common sense view of the day and pedagogic work and activity (Bourdieu, 2000). The opportunity to critique misrecognition that may prevent the reproduction of symbolic violence was limited (Bourdieu, 1994, 2000, 2004) and this arguably presented barriers to social justice. This kind of knowledge agrees with Gunter's (2005): 'delivering change' (p. 170) of Gunter's typology of knowledge with the evaluative and the instrumental being a preferred epistemological approach at this stage. Joanne was located within this first stage.

The second stage of the Learning to CARE model was accessing the thinking tools of critical analysis and reflection. This is where the learners were able to critically analyse and reflect on their learning journeys which altered the way they perceived their practice which was found to be illuminating. At this stage the evidence demonstrates that learners shifted to using this new way of knowing that illuminated their practice. The empirical evidence showed that learners understood that their values, beliefs, behaviours and identities were shifting as a result of new insights they gained in the generation of new knowledge. Learners began to recognize how their capital (Bourdieu, 2000) had changed during their learning journeys and this was both uncomfortable and frustrating. This kind of knowledge connects with Gunter's (2005): 'understanding experiences' (p. 170) on Gunter's typology of knowledge with the humanistic and aesthetic being the preferred epistemological approach. Helen and Antonia were located within this second stage.

The third stage was where the identities of the learners began to settle on their learning journeys and their critical analysis and reflection impacted upon practice in a process of reflexivity. This understanding became consolidated as learners moved beyond resisting how they had colluded in accepting and embedding a deterministic view of structuralist constructivism (Reay, 2004). This means repeating patterns of behaviour and life trajectories that are affirmed through the way in which an individual perceives the world. Their perceptions in turn shape their actions which shape their perceptions of what they can and can not think and do. Thus the reality of the world in the mind becomes the reality external to the world in an iterative relationship. This relationship with the internal self and the external environment might be closed to innovation, or might be open to alternative ways of thinking and doing. Thus a citizen might recognize their role in reproducing and embedding social injustice, or they may remain ignorant of it (Bourdieu, 2000). This kind of knowledge affirms Gunter's (2005): 'understanding meanings' (p. 170) with the conceptual and the descriptive being the favoured epistemological approach. Dasha, Lawrence and Irena were located within this stage as was Helen. This is interesting because Helen was also located in stage 2. This is because the empirical evidence demonstrated that Helen was reflexive in the main but reported that she found it difficult to critique authoritative perspectives because it was part of her taken-for-granted behaviour. This meant that she had not settled into stage 3 yet as she shifted back and forth between stages 2 and 3.

The final stage is the 'move on' stage to emancipation. Here, leaders' reflexivity influences the school community through communicative action underpinned by the democratization of knowledge to generate knowledge that recognizes open systems (Bourdieu, 2000). This begins to remove barriers to social justice in the school community (Ball, 2006). Evidence for this was found with Hannah who stated that she gave a dinner lady the chance to become a school teacher. Jean said that in her secondary school she asked the 'why' questions which afforded colleagues the opportunity to question the common sense view. Henry stated that without critical analysis he made a lot of claims that were not substantiated with evidence, which he suggested were dangerous. Henry continued to articulate that he went to another school that was similar to his in context, but that was performing better. This challenged Henry's understanding of how to lead a school through engaging with evidence informed leadership. He had the opportunity to begin to share this with his community through communicative action. He said that this enabled him to give colleagues opportunities they may not have had before, so that their subjective expectations might begin to meet their objective chances (Bourdieu, 2000).

The leaders who were engaging with communicative action within their educational settings were all at stage four of the Learning to CARE pedagogical tool. The evidence suggests that once the postgraduate researcher had reached this stage 4, they may use the Learning to CARE pedagogical tool to enable them to evaluate how receptive they are to engaging with evidence informed leadership independently, or working collaboratively with their former postgraduate research supervisor. Using the Learning to CARE pedagogical tool in this way gives them the opportunity to map the intellectual tools of critical analysis, reflection and reflexivity in their postgraduate research. This pedagogical tool may then be shared with other members of the community to foster their use of the thinking tools to facilitate evidence informed leadership. This presents a window of opportunity for structural constructivism to remain an open system in school communities underpinned by evidence informed leadership. Hannah, Matthew, Jean, Charlotte and Henry were at this stage 4 of Learning to CARE.

Conclusions

The evidence reveals that the postgraduate research provides educational leaders with opportunities to engage with intellectual work. This enterprise enables them to construct evidence that they could use to make informed decisions in complex educational settings. This met quality frameworks such as the QAA criteria. The evidence reveals that giving leaders access to thinking tools equipped them for evidence informed leadership. Lunt's (2002) mode of critical knowledge was identified as important to facilitate the leaders' ability to critique the commonly held views within their educational institutions and communities. A further thinking tool was that of reflection and Leitch and Day's (2001) pedagogical tool kit was presented to facilitate learners' reflection on their praxis that may lead to a shift in identity (Thomson, 2006). Gunter's typology of knowledge was also identified as important tool to help leaders think about their epistemological approach to their postgraduate research. The leaders' engagement with these thinking tools was mapped using the Learning to CARE pedagogical tool (Taysum, 2006a) which has four stages. The learners at stage 1 are beginning to have access to the thinking tool of critical analysis. The learners at stage 2 are beginning to be critical and reflective, and are gaining new insights into different ways of knowing and doing. The learners at stage 3 are being critical, and reflective and this is impacting upon their practice through a process of reflexivity. Learners at stage 4 are being critical, reflective and reflexive, and are engaging with evidence informed leadership. The leaders at this stage reported that they were able to use evidence informed leadership from postgraduate research to develop their leadership capacity with their school communities. Moreover, they were able to remove barriers to social justice by recognizing parts of individuals' identities that had previously been misrecognized through symbolic violence. The leaders achieved this by providing enhanced educational opportunities for adults as well as students in their educational communities. Therefore, the evidence reveals that postgraduate research equipped educational leaders to begin to meet social justice agendas such as No Child Left Behind and Every Child Matters policy agendas.

I argued that the Learning to CARE pedagogical tool (Taysum, 2006a) is potentially useful because it can help leaders map their development as autonomous researchers. This has the potential to enable them to transform their communities into those that engage with evidence informed leadership. However, it is important to note that Peters (1974) suggests teaching can be defined as both trying to, and succeeding in, imparting that which is worthwhile and *moral* to the learner(s). I recommend that further research be carried out to examine quality in postgraduate research masters and doctoral pedagogies beyond the bounds of this study. This would further develop the research base for the claims made here of sufficient quality to serve what Leithwood, Harris and Hopkins (2008, p. 42) describe as: 'powerful guides to policy and practice'. Such research would also need to address how to frame teaching and learning in postgraduate research that is moral to enable educational leaders to work for civic engagement in their educational communities. This is particularly important if evidence informed leadership is to play a part in removing the barriers to social justice. However, the ethical frameworks for developing evidence informed leadership need to be considered, which is the substance of the next chapter, Chapter 6. Here tensions between who is actively associating with their educational communities and who is marginalized is explored. The role of dialogue is considered as a method for how communities might contribute to the interpretation of policies and structures that shape their lives. How communities might use dialogue to reach provisional consensus is explored. To do this, dialogue builds on discourses that examine issues surrounding positionality, dispositions and what it means to search for truth while reconciling issues of power among different cultures. Here the notion of ethical evidence informed leadership is brought into sharp focus.

References

Ball, S. J. (2006), *Education Policy and Social Class*. London: Routledge.
Barnett, R. (1997), *Higher Education: A critical business*. Buckingham: SRHE/OUP.
Bourdieu, P. (1994), *In Other Words. Essays towards a reflexive society*. Cambridge: Polity.
—— (2000), *Pascalian Meditations*. Cambridge: Polity.
—— (2004), *The Field of Cultural Production*. Cambridge: Polity.
Cribb, A. and Gewirtz, S. (2003), Towards a sociology of just practices; an analysis of plural conceptions of justice. In C. Vincent (ed.), *Social Justice Education and Identity* (pp. 15–29). London: RoutledgeFalmer.
Delanty, G. (2001), *Challenging Knowledge: The university in the knowledge society*. Buckingham: SRHE and Open University Press.
Flessa, J. (2007), The trouble with the EdD. *Leadership and Policy in Schools*, 6, 197–208.
Gandin, L. and Apple, M. (2002), Challenging neo-liberalism building a democracy: creating the citizen school in Porto Alegre Brazil. *Journal of Education Policy*, 17 (2), 259–79.
Grenfell, M., James, D., Reay, D. and Robbins, D. (1998), *Bourdieu and Education: Acts of practical theory*. Oxon: Falmer Press.
Gunter, H. (2005), Conceptualising research in educational leadership. *Educational Management Administration and Leadership*, 33 (2), 165–80.
Hall, V. (1998), We are all adult educators now: the implications of Adult Learning Theory for the continuing professional development of educational leaders and managers. *ESRC Seminar Series: Redefining educational management*. Milton Keynes, England.
Hodgkinson, C. (1991), *Educational Leadership: The moral art*. Albany: State University of New York Press.
Leitch, R. and Day, C. (2001) Reflective processes in action: mapping personal and professional contexts for learning and change. *Journal of In-Service Education*, 27 (2), 237–59.

Leithwood, K., Harris, A., and Hopkins, D. (2008). Seven strong claims about effective school leadership. In School Leadership and Management, 28 (1), 27–42.

Levine, A. (2005), *Educating School Leaders.* New York: Education Schools Project.

Luke, A. (2006), Teaching after the market from commodity to cosmopolitan. In L. Weis, G. McCarthy and G. Dimitriadis (eds), *Ideology, Curriculum and the New Sociology of Education Revisiting the Work of Michael Apple.* London: Routledge.

Lunt, I. (2002), *Integrating Academic and Professional Knowledge: Constructing the practitioner-researcher.* Available from: http://www.qut.edu.au/dresa/CPE/ProfDocs/Papers/Scott_paper.doc (accessed 4 March 2003).

Middleton, S. (2007), The place of theory: locating the New Zealand 'education' Ph.D. experience 1948–1998. *British Journal of Sociology of Education,* 28 (1), 69–87.

Nash, R. (1999), Bourdieu, 'habitus' and educational research: is it all worth the candle? *British Journal of Sociology of Education,* 20 (2), 175–187.

Peters, R. (1974), *Ethics and Education.* London: Unwin University Books.

—— (1977), *Authority, Responsibility and Education.* London: George Allen and Unwin.

Pring, R. (2005), *Philosophy of Education* (QAA) London: Continuum.

Quality Assurance Agency for Higher Education. (2007), *The Framework for Higher Education Qualifications in England Wales and Northern Ireland.* Available from: http://www.qaa.ac.uk/academicinfrastructure/FHEQ/EWNI/default.asp (accessed 2007).

—— (2008), *The Framework for Higher Education Qualifications in England, Wales and Northern Ireland.* Mansfield: Lenney Direct.

Reay, D. (2004), It's all becoming habitus: beyond the habitual use of habitus in educational research. *British Journal of Sociology,* 4, 431–44.

Reay, D. and Arnot, M. (2004). Participation and Control in Learning: a Pedagogic Democratic Right? In C. Vincent, Learning to Read Critically in Teaching and Learning. London, Sage.

Ross, A. (2000), *Curriculum Construction and Critique.* London: Falmer Press.

Schilling, C. (2004), Physical capital and situated action: a new direction for corporeal sociology. *British Journal of Sociology of Education,* 25 (4), 473–87.

Scott, D., Brown, A., Lunt, I. and Thorne, L. (2004), *Professional Doctorates Integrating Professional and Academic Knowledge.* Berkshire: The Open University Press.

Taysum, A. (2006a), *A survey of the learning journeys of school leaders doing the Doctorate of Education in England.* Birmingham: University of Birmingham.

—— (2006b), The distinctiveness of the EdD within the university tradition. Journal of Education Administration and History, 38 (3), 323–34.

Taysum, A. (2008), The role of research in developing Educational Leadership for the 21st century: creating our future. *British Educational Leadership Management, and Administration Society Symposium.* American Educational Research Association Annual Conference, New York.

Taysum, A. and Gunter, H. (2008), A critical approach to researching social justice and school leadership in England. *Education, Citizenship and Social Justice,* 3 (2), 183–99.

Thomson, P. (2006), Miners, diggers, ferals and showmen: school-community projects that affirm and unsettle identities and place. *British Journal of Sociology of Education,* 27 (1), 81–96.

Chapter 6

Ethical Frameworks for Developing Evidence Informed Leadership

The sixth chapter explores the tensions between who is actively associating with their educational communities, and who is marginalized. The role of dialogue is explored as a method for how communities might contribute to the interpretation of policies and structures that shape their lives. How communities might use dialogue to reach provisional consensus is explored. To do this, dialogue builds on discourses that examine issues surrounding positionality, dispositions and what it means to search for truth while reconciling issues of power among different cultures. Here the notion of evidence informed leadership in education is considered in terms of guarding against 'false and dangerous promises' and the need for such leadership to be ethical.

Who is actively associating with educational communities?

Through democracy citizens have the chance to participate in the selection of the policies that shape their lives. This is usually achieved through democratic elections. However, the notion of democracy and social justice needs to be interrogated as identified in chapter two when Shields (2007) argues that the notion of democracy can be inadequate. The case study Shields presents revealed that 75 per cent of the parent population did not attend the meeting to vote. The non-attendees represented the disadvantaged school population. A reason given for their non-attendance was that they take several jobs to try to keep up. The demands on their time to earn a living and 'keep up' prevented them from attending the meeting. Moreover, taking several jobs potentially prevented them from supporting their children's learning such as reading to them. However, this positioning is interpreted by the superintendent and the board as lack of interest in their children's education. This claim was evidenced by the 'democratic' vote against the change in school calendar. Yet the principal acknowledged that the proposed reform to the school calendar had failed without being given a chance. The notion of 'so-called democracy' appears inadequate in this case if democracy is defined as a minority deciding for the majority. The notion of democracy and its relationship with dominant discourses, knowledge and power needs to be interrogated. Shields (2007) provides some activities based on the case study to help educational leaders do this and this is based on critiquing and reflecting upon dominant discourses as discussed in chapters 4 and 5.

Dialogue is an important form of communication to begin to understand the extent to which people are able to recognize the practice and thinking of others, particularly those of minority or marginalized communities. To be able to recognize minority and marginalized community groups it is important to engage with community dialogue to begin to gain a deeper understanding of the different groups that make up a community. This is an important first step and one that appears to be missing in the democratic voting that occurred in the case study Shields (2007) presents. Facilitating dialogue is the first and important step that enables an educational leader to work on behalf of those least advantaged in society and educational systems without pathologizing or essentializing them. The educational leader who engages with dialogue may find what they hear uncomfortable because they may realize they have unwittingly been part of the misrecognition of minority and marginalized communities. On the other hand, an educational leader who works within structures of high levels of public accountability with high-stakes tests, may feel unable to start dialogues. In this scenario the leaders collude with dominant discourses. McDermott (2007) argues such dominant discourses frequently rehearse blaming the marginalized for their marginalization and argues that the testing regimes that are part of the No Child Left Behind policy agenda in the United States identify marginalized students as failures at a very early stage in their young lives. In this scenario, the children who are the future never feel 'good enough'. They may desire to be good enough, but they can not be good enough which leads to angst. Angst is when a person is at odds with themselves, and this is an uncomfortable position to be in, particularly for young children who are vulnerable members of society who look to adults to protect them. Therefore, an education system potentially exists that pathologizes minority groups by testing to prove (whether intentionally or not) they are, or are not good enough. Such an approach to education is not going to prepare the next generation to be the best they can be, or as Maslow describes it, to 'self actualize'. Such practice leads to the children having low self-esteem which will have effects on their behaviour in society which Bernstein examines in his theories about sub-groups. Here, children are labelled as failing and therefore the only way they can get a sense of achievement is from achieving and excelling at 'not being good'. The learners may do this through risky or bad behaviour since that is all that they can be recognized for being good at. This argument has implications for the social justice agendas of Every Child Matters in England and the No Child Left Behind in the United States, and the ongoing debate of the usefulness of high-stakes testing in schools. It is interesting to note that the National Union of Teachers and the National Association of Head Teachers Union, two major teacher unions in England considered boycotting Statutory Assessment Tests (SATs) in primary schools because they were putting too much stress on children (Curtis, 2009). The arguments for preventing an attack on a child's self-esteem are even more compelling because the learners are developing a sense of self during their education. Developing a sense of self within educational systems that label the most vulnerable members of society as failures is an example of what Bourdieu (2000) calls symbolic violence and is therefore abusive. Whether the structures are intended to adversely affect a child's well-being or not, this is the effect.

As stated in Chapter 2, Rowland (2008) cites a report on 14th February 2007 from the United Nations Children's Fund positioned the United States and Great Britain as the worst two countries in the industrialized global village in which to be a child. UNICEF examined 40 factors including poverty, deprivation, happiness, relationships, and risky or bad behaviour. In a table of 21 economically developed nations, the United States and Great Britain came 20th and 21st respectively. Such evidence further substantiates the need for educational leaders to engage with the Learning to CARE framework provided in Chapter 5 by critiquing and reflecting upon the evidence from their postgraduate research and transforming their practice to improve the situation. Such evidence informed leadership facilitates confronting the 'common sense view'. If this does not occur the inequities may become more deeply embedded in current and future generations through policy or case law. Such legislation is very often developed to actually remove barriers to social justice, but fails because it does not contain the necessary codes, networks of classification, symbolic activity and shared meanings to recognize minority and marginalized communities (Strain, 1998). Without such recognition policies and law may enable the taken-for-granted to bore more deeply into education systems and education policy. Ethical leaders need to be democratic in decision making, and they need to listen to young people – which they can be bad at. It is a moral imperative to engage in dialogue with all those on whose behalf they are taking decisions.

The importance of dialogue in communication

Brighouse and Woods (1999) state, 'We remain impressed by schools which are eternally attending to improvements in communication in a systematic way' (p. 14). Good dialogue is important to develop a shared sense of meaning. This approach is echoed by Stoll *et al.* (2003), who suggest that community dialogue enables a shared sense of meaning 'about where you are going as a school and working to adapt your goals in the light of messages from your context' (p. 142). Dialogue also enables individuals to explore their values and beliefs and engage with the messy process of how these connect with the values and beliefs of the community. This resonates with Hedges (1985), who suggests dialogue 'often helps people to analyse their own attitudes, ideas and beliefs and behaviour more penetratingly' (p. 73). Arguably dialogue of this quality, if underpinned by respect for agents in an environment of trust would facilitate learning. Indeed, Southworth (2004) argues that talk can lead to experiential learning that supports 'professional knowledge that is explicit, practical and applicable. It is the kind of knowledge teachers value and crave' (p. 109).

Space needs to be created for dialogue so that educational leaders can begin to engage in civic work with their communities. This space needs to be free, so that participants are able to take the time to make meaningful and worthwhile contributions to the dialogue. Free space enables the participants to take the time to listen deeply and to reach a provisional consensus together.

Reaching a provisional consensus

A provisional consensus is one found in Socratic dialogue, where the belief that there is one truth is acknowledged to be the root of evil. This does not mean that truth does not exist. What it means is that the search for truth underpins the critical understanding of the self (Heckmann, 2004). It is important to note that Socratic dialogue, is not the sole way of trying to reach a provisional consensus. To get to the point of provisional consensus the participants of the dialogue listen deeply to each other. Leal and Saran (2004) argue that the kind of *dialogue* required to engage with such issues needs to focus on deep listening and trying to understand one another. This is important when addressing the goals of institutional improvement and the problems that are inherent in institutions' specific contexts. Leaders potentially need to consider different ways of thinking about the goals of their educational institutions, and ways of behaving to meet the goals. Leal and Saran (2004) argue that taking time to listen deeply during dialogues to try to reach understandings of all group members' perspectives is important. However, such an approach to dialogue can be lost because individuals can feel frustrated if they do not get to an answer quickly. Indeed Leal and Saran (2004) suggest that rushing to an answer prevents the deep listening required that provides opportunities to explore alternative possibilities.

Thus dialogues that include deep listening may develop over time, and do not provide quick answers to complex problems. Through such social interactions identities are formed that do not exist in isolation. This notion is found in South Africa's notion of 'Ubuntu', which is a position in the group of 'I am because we exist'. Ubuntu means that the group subordinate their egos for the common or public good of the group to ensure successful survival together (De Liefde, 2007). Leaders working for social justice recognize that being part of a dialogue is very different to educational communities listening to monologues from educational leaders, and passively receiving transmitted knowledge that they are not a part of co-constructing. Dominant voices skew structural constructivism which is a barrier to more socially just democratic structural constructivism from coming to be.

Achieving provisional consensus

To achieve provisional consensus through Socratic dialogue, Leal and Saran (2004) argue that there are three basic aims. First, to answer a question by seeking the truth and coming to a provisional consensus. Second, to cooperate with the participants of the group and to understand each other by engaging fully and honestly in the dialogue process. Finally, to gain deeper insights and understandings of values, and moral issues to form the basis for social action and to live a good life. Such dialogues have the potential to enhance self-confidence as participants recognize that they can deal rationally with their emotions through reason. Such self-awareness connects with the important concept of what Socrates called 'know yourself inscribed [*sic*] at the temple at Delphi' cited in Beck (2003). Gaining self-awareness, and self-confidence may predicate gaining self-esteem so that participants recognize that they are good enough. Feeling good enough may be the bedrock for good social behaviour so that students can be recognized for good behaviour which they are good at rather than recognized for bad or risky behaviour. This has implications for improving the placings of the United States and Great Britain in any future report from the United Nations International Children's Fund. It is interesting to note that while the high-stakes testing systems label the children as not being good enough, the countries that have these high-stakes tests are also identified by UNICEF (2007) as not being good enough at developing the next generation.

It is important to engage in dialogue about moral issues so that all members of the community are able to take the knowledge that they have learned and compare and contrast it with their values systems, and the value systems of others. This potentially enables them to gain understanding of the self and others which may underpin making decisions about what is good and what is bad. Learning about the self and others in this way may also enable communities to become more tolerant of each other. Ultimately this enables the individual and the community to balance making choices about how to live a good life together in peace. Using the philosophy of Ubuntu may enable groups to learn about how to live a good life together for the public good. For this to occur the notion of 'good' and 'bad' or 'right' and 'wrong' needs to be considered.

Moral values and purposes underlying the notion of 'good' and 'bad'

Leaders need to be able to have both a clear sense of right and wrong and communicate this clearly with their communities. They also need to role model the 'right' behaviour and expect 'right' behaviour from others that exemplifies professional ethics.

Pring (2000) suggests professional ethics are a search for rules for right thought and right behaviour. This is more than just doing the right thing, it is also having the right kind of thinking. In other words, ethics is a search for rules to understand what is moral and what is immoral. Trying to work this out is very difficult and calls for universal ethical principles that can be applied in all situations. Such universal principles have three different elements at their centre. The first is consequences, the second rights, and the third virtues (Pring, 2000).

Consequences are the good or bad results of an action, the good effects are moral actions and the bad effects are immoral actions. Morally right actions yield the best consequences for all. Thinking through how action and thought may have the best possible processes and results for everyone is what John Stuart Mill called the utility principle (Sher, 2001). Inclusion where all participants have equality of opportunity to take part may be a goal of the whole community. On the other hand, when the results of an action are thought of only in terms of moral duties to the self, it can be said that this is egotistical which is the antithesis of 'Ubuntu'. A different way of considering ethics is the way people treat each other which may be thought of in terms of individual rights and societal rights. Action can be said to be moral when it respects the rights of the self, and of another, and immoral if it does not. However, in all communities it is important to remember that with respect and rights for persons, comes *responsibilities*. Ethical principles may also focus on moral virtues. These may be habitual attributes or traits of a person. Gronn (2003) warns about the heroic man who may lead in settings in an undemocratic manner. Grace (1995) also warns against being unrealistic and hoping for 'salvationist leadership' to overcome moral, economic and social problems. It is also important to consider that having unrealistic expectations can lead to demotivation and stress (Earley *et al.*, 2002).

Moral virtues may be exposed when an individual reacts to a particular situation. Jones and McNamee (2000) suggest that a reaction to a situation may call for moral virtues such as: 'courage, compassion, determination, honesty, loyalty or fairness' (p. 143). The virtues needed by a person will not be known before the event and, therefore, cannot be planned for.

Moral leadership in particular communities or organizations could be said to be about thinking about and doing the right thing. Leaders need to be aware that others may have different ideas about 'right thought and right action'. Therefore, being a moral leader may be trying to find the moral balance for individuals and the group. Building these kinds of relationships is important in moral leadership and trust needs to be won. From this starting point, people may begin to trust others and in turn become worthy of trust. Arguably, in dialogues trust is vital and involves overcoming anxiety at taking risks when moving forward into the unknown. Trust then is about the process not just the consequences of action. Trust in relationships may have aspects such as faithfulness, loyalty, sacrifice and sharing. Sharing may include that of information, jobs, and maintaining confidentiality. The testing of trust may be done publicly or privately. An example of a public test may be through inspections. An example of a private test may be through appraisal where competence and commitment may be scrutinized.

As stated previously trust does not just 'happen' it needs to be developed, and affirmed by leaders in various ways through the demonstration of moral values that informs the behaviour of leaders who may role model moral values for the community. This resonates with how John Locke describes a leader who is a wise person, who both develops and role models good habits. Habitually making decisions in this way may lead to moment-to-moment authentic decision making. This may flow between the science and art of pedagogy or pedagogic work (Luke, 2006). Such democratic authentic evidence informed leadership might be found in relationships between the various members of an educational community, and the processes or structures that enable this to happen smoothly.

Developing citizens to approach and engage with civic work through dialogue

Taysum (2008) argues that civic education and educating for the human *good* requires thinking through communities' most noble and highest aims (Collins, 2004). These aims then need to be subject to rigorous critique and presented to citizens for them to critique and discuss. As I identified earlier, it is very important that each individual has the opportunity to have his or her voice heard in such debates because the outcomes of the debates at civic level will shape what individuals and the community can and can not do. As Shields (2007) identified it is important that the individuals are aware of when the debates are taking place, that they have a place at the debate, and that they can physically attend given their personal circumstances that might include having three jobs. It is troubling that citizens may not know how to take part in civic engagement, and it is troubling if individuals do not know why it is important that they are involved in civic engagement. At a very basic level, Faulks (2006) identifies that there was a 61 per cent voter turn out in the 2005 general election in Britain. If citizens are not engaging with voting, it is unlikely that they will be engaging with debates at the civic level. Perhaps educational leaders doing postgraduate research may be able to help individuals and the community to recognize the implications for their lives if they include themselves in civic debates, or enable them to articulate what de-selecting taking part in civic debates means for their lives. Moreover, they need to be able to explain what collusion in their own exclusion means in terms of being part of, or not being part of the co-construction of knowledge and/or policy that shapes what they can and can not know and do now and in the future. In other words, people need to be able to describe and understand what structural constructivism is in closed deterministic systems and what structural constructivism is in open systems. They then need to make informed choices about which system they want to be a part of and how they become a part of that particular system through civic work. Finally, they need to be able to understand and explain why they are involved with civic work and how this might relate to right behaviour or good behaviour that is recognized as 'good enough'.

Citizens need the tools to be able to critically and reflectively consider the economic and cultural capital so that they can make choices about how they will engage with the civic work democratically. By this I mean that they will recognize their own *rights*, and take *responsibility* when exercising those rights. Taysum (2008) cites Aristotle's argument that the central role of philosophy is to critique the challenges of public and social life. This needs to be done ethically and frameworks have been developed for helping people to think about how their moral values might inform their behaviour. Jones and McNamee (2000) have developed such a framework from Kohlberg's classical development of moral judgement for sports contexts. They argue that those of mature moral character are able to choose the right thing to do from impartial moral rules and principles. Morally mature judgements come from a framework that helps to think through the values in organizations in terms of justice. The framework comes from research from different countries and a range of cultures. The research shows that people develop their ability to take moral decisions that shape their moral actions over their learning journeys that can take place over a lifetime. They describe three levels and six stages that people pass through on their learning journeys to moral maturity. Kohlberg's adapted framework is presented in Table 1.

At stage 1 of the framework, the good or bad thing to do is shaped by the desire to be obedient and to avoid punishment, and this comes from fear of getting into trouble. At stage 2, people are motivated by enhancing their self-interests and they are working at a level that Kohlberg describes as pre-conventional. This means that people at these two stages are not yet thinking about society or institutional moral conventions – or responsibilities, rather they are thinking about themselves. At stage 3, people behave morally to be accepted, or liked by particular groups, cultures, or societies. At stage 4, people begin to recognize the importance of responsibilities and behave morally not just out of fear of being punished but because they want to do their duty as a good citizen. These levels are at the 'conventional' level where moral duty to community convention takes priority. Those at stage 5 see the government as a legal body not a moral one, believing a higher moral authority exists based on societal first principles and values. Individuals at stage 5 believe the government should serve the people and if they are not serving the people's best interests then they need to be challenged, and even changed. Here the moral purpose is equal human rights where all are valued and afforded dignity, and self-worth. People at stage 6 will rise above the

Table 1 Jones and McNamee's (2000, p.133) levels of moral development (adapted from Kohlberg, 1981, pp. 17–19).

(i) *The Pre-conventional Level*	*The self is the primary concern in moral considerations*
Stage 1. Punishment and obedience orientation	Obedience is valued in its own right and the goodness of an action is determined by its physical consequences
Stage 2. The instrumental relative orientation	Value is judged in terms of instrumental worth to the self. There is an 'eye for an eye' conception of justice
(ii) *Conventional level*	*The morality of the given convention or society is adopted*
Stage 3. The interpersonal concordance level	Persons conform to their perception of the social norm
Stage 4. Society maintaining orientation	Rules and norms of society are respected and give rise to certain duties
(iii) *Post-conventional or principled level*	*Moral judgements are universal and Impartial*
Stage 5. The stage of prior rights or social contract	The morally right thing to do is still determined by norms and rules, however persons are actively involved in their construction
Stage 6. The stage of universal ethical principles	A concern for universal ethical principles guides all action

conventional values of society to realize universal ethical principles. Those working at stage 5 and 6 are at a post-conventional level and can transcend concerns of the self and of the society if the societal values are flawed and not working for the people's dignity and equal human rights. This framework is useful to help think through the kinds of decisions leaders might make.

However, this framework is limited in sports contexts since frequently immoral action is found in foul play and illegal tactics. These things enhance self/team interests, but it is hard to work out what is moral or immoral from observations, as umpires/referees will testify. It is also very difficult to make such judgements in sports contexts when such actions are made in split seconds when there is very little time for thinking through consequences of actions. Therefore, Jones and McNamee present Haan's framework that looks at moral dialogue for the development of moral character and this connection is important for this research. Haan (1978) believes that the development of moral maturity can occur when people examine concrete situations and discuss the evidence rather than consider made up situations.

In this framework there are three phases with different levels at each phase. The first phase is assimilation where power balancing is negotiated. Here compromise is sought, but with the interest of the self at the centre of the negotiations. The second phase is accommodation where the dialogue tries to sustain the group's moral balance. The third phase is harmony balancing, where there is recognition that the group interests are no different from the interests of the self. The fourth level is common interest balancing, where the moral balance is negotiated for both the self and the group, and these interests are recognized to be potentially different. The final level is that of equilibrium where all interests lead to moral balance in all situations. Using such frameworks, and having the thinking tools to engage critically with such frameworks may enable engagement with civic work to address economic and social inequalities.

Building trust

When engaging in dialogue for civic work, it is important to facilitate the building of trust between the participants of the community. Engaging with evidence

Table 2 Haan's phases and levels of maturity (adapted from Haan, 1978, pp. 288–89).

(i) *Assimilation phase*	*Seek moral balances that benefit the self*
Level 1. Power balancing	Balances are negotiated to reflect self-interest
Level 2. Egocentric balancing	Acknowledgement of others interests but compromises only occur when benefit the self
(ii) *Accomodation phase*	*Seek to maintain a moral balance for the group*
Level 3. Harmony balancing	Recognition of group interests but perceived as no different from self-interest
Level 4. Common interest balancing	Persons differentiate self-interest and group interest and seek balances to maintain group norms
(iii) *Equilibrium phase*	*Seek to optimize everyone's interests impartially*
Level 5. Mutual interest balancing	Recognition of the necessity of moral balances to optimize the interests of all in all situations

informed leadership means that conclusions and recommendations upon which decisions are made need to be specific, measurable, achievable, realistic and time bound. If they are not then the participants of the dialogue may lose trust in the process of dialogue. This is potentially very dangerous because it sets a standard against which future dialogues will be measured. If participants believe the dialogue process to be untrustworthy, then they may not engage with future dialogues. The damage this might have on the community and its engagement with research and evidence informed leadership could have far-reaching effects and may even affirm a 'not good enough' self-perception. Here a participant who is recognized as not good enough may think they are not worthy to be treated with respect, and therefore collude in their own exclusion by being good at 'risky or bad behaviour' which undermines striving for inclusionary civic work.

In summary, there are tensions between who is actively associating with their educational communities, and who is marginalized. The notion of democracy needs to be redefined in terms of inclusion. This means that there are equality of opportunities to contribute to the decision making processes that shape the 'I and the we'. The role of dialogue was presented as an important way of enabling community members to contribute to the interpretation of policies and structures that shape their lives. Such dialogues would need to be taken step by step in a cooperative and trusting context where communities have the chance to reach provisional consensus before moving on to the next step. Such a method enables participants to examine their own values' systems in relation to the topic or issue of the dialogue. For dialogue to work the participants need to search for the truth while reconciling issues of power among different cultures. Understanding and respecting tolerance is important here so that the notion of evidence informed leadership is considered in terms of facilitating the building of trust between participants. If dialogue occurs under these conditions there is an opportunity to gain understanding within the community, which is an important step towards finding solutions to problems. Educational communities need opportunities for people to address the problems of public life through dialogue with critical reflection. The thinking tools of being critical and reflective are those that the educational leaders gain and/or enhance during postgraduate research so that they can engage with evidence informed leadership. Educational leaders need to lead teachers and their communities in communication through dialogue to think through how they will approach and engage with solving problems of public life and social life in their educational communities. Using frameworks that explore the balance between the self and society, or the 'I and the we' (Ubuntu) citizens can think through the kinds of relationships needed for such civic work. Moreover, these issues can be examined in the classroom where there is free space for dialogue. Here the emotional, or affective domain should not be skipped over in favour of the cognitive. Beatty (2007) makes the claim that emotional experiences inform the development of personal, social, cultural, and political processes and relationships. Therefore, community leaders laying the foundations for building inclusionary relationships of trust and opportunity for cooperative dialogue for civic work need to do so with humility, honesty and criticality. Thus in educational institutions, communities may practice building relationships with each other that may continue to develop, refresh and sustain day by day (Beatty, 2007) with a sharp focus on economic and cultural justice located in a world that is able to enjoy ecological equilibrium that is self-sustaining.

References

Beatty, B. (2007), Going through the emotions: leadership that gets to the heart of school renewal. *Australian Journal of Education*, 51 (3), 328–40.

Beck, S. (2003), *Socrates Know Yourself.* Available at: http://www.san.beck.org.SOC1-Know Yourself.html (accessed 4 August 2003).

Bourdieu, P. (2000), *Pascalian Meditations.* Cambridge: Polity.

Brighouse, T. and Woods, D. (2003), *How to Improve Your School.* London: Routledge.

Collins, S. (2004), Moral virtue and the limits of the political community in Artistotle's Nichomachean Ethics. *American Journal of Political Science*, 48 (1), 47–61.

Curtis, P. (2009), Education Unions plan 2010 Sats boycott. *Guardian*, 26 March. [online]. Available at: http://www.guardian.co.uk/education/2009/mar/26/education-unions-exams (accessed 24 May 2010).

De Liefde W. H. J. (2007), *Lekgotla.* South Africa: Jacana.

Earley, P., Evans, J., Collarbone, P., Gold, A. and Halpin, D. (n.d.), *Establishing the Current State of School Leadership in England.* Available at: http://www.dfes.gov.uk/research/data/uploadfiles/RR336.pdf (accessed 15 December 2002).

Faulkes, K. (2006), Rethinking citizenship education in England some lessons from contemporary social and political theory. *Education, Citizenship and Social Justice*, 1 (2), 123–40.

Grace, G. (1995), *School Leadership Beyond Education Management: An essay in policy scholarship.* London: The Falmer Press.

Gronn, P. (2003), *The New Work of Educational Leaders.* London: Sage.

Haan, N. (1978), Two moralities in action contexts: relationship to thought, ego, regulation, and development. *Journal of Personality and Social Psychology*, 36, 286–305.

Heckmann, G. (2004), Six pedagogical measures and Socratic facilitation. In R. Saran and B. Neisser (eds), *Enquiring Minds.* Stoke-on-Trent: Trentham Books.

Hedges, L. V. (1985), Does money matter? A meta-analysis of studies of the effects of differential school inputs on student outcomes (an exchange: Part 1). *Educational Researcher*, 23 (3), 5–14.

Jones, C. and McNamee, M. (2000), Sports, ethics and philosophy; context, history, prospects. *Sport, Ethics and Philosophy*, 1 (1), 131–46.

Kohlberg, L. (1981), *Essays on Moral Development, Vol. I: The philosophy of moral development.* San Francisco, CA: Harper & Row.

Leal, F. and Saran, R. (2004), A dialogue on the Socratic dialogue, act two. In P. Shipley (ed.), *Occasional Working Papers in Ethics and Critical Philosophy*, 3.

Luke, A. (2006), Teaching after the market from commodity to cosmopolitan. In L. Weis, G. McCarthy and G. Dimitriadis, Ideology, curriculum and the new sociology of education revisiting the work of Michael Apple. London: Routledge.

McDermott, K. (2007), 'Expanding the moral community' or 'blaming the victim'? The politics of state education accountability policy. *American Educational Research Journal*, 44 (1), 77–111.

Pring, R. (2000), *Philosophy of Educational Research*. London: Continuum.

Rowland, K. (2008) Freedom, Inclusion, Interaction, and Growth; Let the Children Fly, in Taysum, A. (Convener and Chair) All Children Matter: Addressing Special and Inclusive Education. Key Note Panel. British Educational Leadership Management, and Administration Society.

Shields, C. (2007), A failed initiative: democracy has spoken – or has it? *Journal of Cases in Educational Leadership*, 10 (1), 14–21.

Saran, R. and Neisser, B. (eds) (2004), *Enquiring Minds*. Stoke-on-Trent: Trentham Books.

Sher, G. (2001), *John Stuart Mill Utilitarianism*. Indianapolis: Hackett Publishing.

Stoll, L., Fink, D. and Earl, L. (2003), *It's About Learning (and it's About Time) What's in it for schools?* London: RoutledgeFalmer.

Southworth, G. (2004a), A response from the National College of School Leadership. *Educational, Management, Leadership and Administration*, 32 (3), 339–54.

Strain, M. (1998), Educational managers' knowledge: the quest for useful theory. In M. Strain, B. Dennison, J. Ouston and V. Hall (eds), *Policy, Leadership and Professional Knowledge in Education*. London: Paul Chapman Publishing.

Taysum, A. (2006b), The distinctiveness of the EdD within the university tradition. *Journal of Education Administration and History*, 38 (3), 323–34.

—— (2008), The role of research in developing educational leadership for the 21st century. *American Educational Research Association Annual Conference*. New York, USA.

United Nations International Children's Fund (2007), Child poverty in perspective: An overview of child well-being in rich countries. Florence: The United Nations Children's Fund.

Chapter 7

Practical Cases Where Evidence Informed Leadership Enhanced Educational Opportunities While Meeting the Social Justice Agenda of Educational Policies

This chapter brings the strands of the first six chapters together. The argument I have made is that through research undertaken in communities of practice supported by the academy, educational leaders are presented with the opportunity to develop a systematic, critical reflective and reflexive approach to policy. This reflexivity becomes evidence informed leadership. I have explained what is meant by this and have shown how such a way of thinking and behaving, underpins informed judgements about praxis in complex settings. I have presented evidence from the field of how educational leaders have developed while engaging in postgraduate research so that they are able to work for social justice in their schools. The importance of engaging with educational communities has been examined, with a sharp focus on facilitating civic engagement with culturally relevant curriculums that are meaningful and worthwhile to all stakeholders. This moves beyond the staff and students to all community members including parents, and policy implementers at district level and policy makers at national level. The role of good communication, particularly through dialogue was highlighted in the previous chapter. I now present evidence from the field that reveals how educational leaders have used postgraduate research to work for social justice. Evidence is presented about how educational leaders' reflexive research has caused transformation of identity (Delamont and Atkinson, 2004). The evidence also shows how reflexive research enhances educational opportunities while meeting social justice agendas contained within policies such as Every Child Matters, No Child Left Behind, and the 'Russian Education – 2020: a model of education for an economy based on knowledge' (2008 [in Russian]).

Addressing barriers to economic and social inequalities, and sustainable living

In Chapter 2 I used Cribb and Gewirtz's (2003) three elements of social just-ice to help think through how educational leaders may be able to facilitate civic engagement within their educational communities. These elements are distributive justice, cultural justice and associational justice. Distributive justice is concerned with the economic which is analysed under three separate subhead-ings; exploitation, economic marginalization, and deprivation. Cultural justice is where there is recognition (Bourdieu, 2000) and respect of all cultures with tolerance being at one end of a continuum and celebration of diversity at the other. Associational justice is where citizens are able to democratically engage with civic work and the decision-making process of how civic work is executed. Civic work and achieving associational justice requires individuals to enjoy equal rights and responsibilities in the choices made that affect their lives. Associational justice therefore engages with how communities might begin to take part in the process of converting policy as text, into policy as discourse. The associational justice element is now drawn upon to theorize what the edu-cational leaders in the researches I have undertaken have said about the ways postgraduate research has enabled them to develop as leaders, as human beings, and to work for social justice. The educational leaders interviewed said that doing postgraduate research enabled them to recognize ways in which they were prejudiced. This enabled them to use their new critical, reflective and reflexive thinking tools described in Chapter 5 to work for social justice. I now reveal the kinds of insights into the self that the educational leaders gained through being critical, reflective and reflexive. Ways in which this may have enabled them to identify 'angst' as described in Chapter 6 is also revealed. By taking a good hard look at internal conflicts that may arise through self-knowledge, the educational leaders are potentially able to recognize 'internal conflicts' or 'angst' not only in their own lives, but in the lives of those they serve. I then show how the leaders used these new ways of thinking and doing to work for social justice. I also reveal some of the postgraduate research programme providers' percep-tions of the educational leaders' transformation during their learning journeys doing postgraduate research, made possible by moving communities towards a situation where all cultures are recognized and respected. However, recognizing different cultures without enabling individuals from those cultures to make democratic contributions towards resolutions that influence them is potentially unjust. Therefore 'associational justice' needs to be an authentic and inclusive process. In Chapter 6, the importance of dialogue in this process was examined. All the leaders I interviewed indicated the importance of dialogue. However, in this chapter, I reveal how a few of the educational leaders have used dialogue to enable educational community members to associate with the knowledge construction that shapes what they can and can not know and do.

Recognizing prejudice within the self, dealing with the resulting angst, and moving closer to authentic recognition of all community members

The ways in which engaging with postgraduate research enabled educational leaders to recognize ways in which they were prejudiced, deal with any angst, and use new insights to work for social justice in their own communities, was unique to each respondent and their context. However, the educational leaders worked hard to recognize members of their communities and to enable them to associate with the policies and structures that shaped what they can and can not think and do. I have already discussed in a paper with Professor Helen Gunter how educational leaders in England engaged with this process in their own lived lives (Taysum and Gunter, 2008). In this chapter the evidence reveals that postgraduate research facilitates such self-knowledge for the educational leaders in the United States, England and Russia. Richard, a leader who works in a district in the United States, says that he grew up in a white, middle-class environment and had little personal experience of the kinds of issues that minority and marginalized groups might face. Richard perceives that his EdD postgraduate research programme enabled him to gain insights into how he was prejudiced and did not realize it because his construction of reality did not include what life is like for marginalized or minority groups. Richard states of his learning on the postgraduate research programe:

In terms of the social justice piece, that was a little eye-opening. The social justice made me a little bit more in touch with my inner prejudices, some of my prejudices, not all of them and not always to what level they affected the decisions that I make, but it did sensitize me to that. The programme was really focused around issues of social justice . . . that was part of what I liked about it . . . my high school had 85 students all but one were Caucasian or Western European we had one Indian student that was it in terms of ethnic diversity, so when I went to college I went to a not really diverse campus for two years then went to another [name of place] where it was mostly white, 80–90 per cent white. In terms of my background, in terms of diversity and sensitivity to the issues of justice and social inequalities, it was fairly limited . . . Yes I am here working in a fairly diverse district. In a lot of ways it is fairly diverse for [name of state]. It is fairly affluent. We have a small population in [name of place] who are low socio-economic status and our minority groups are actually some of our stronger groups sometimes so our Indian population or Asian population are doing well our Afro Americans struggle Hispanics struggle . . . our Afro-American groups are only a small percentage of the population, so it is really our Hispanic population that is the largest group that struggles. My exposure to that was fairly limited. I was teaching in high schools like my high school with a white majority, and even in my role now I don't deal with kids. I deal with mostly teachers and my teachers are mostly white, fairly well off. So my work context was not going to really challenge me much and the leadership here wasn't really hugely sensitive to those kinds of issues . . . So it was good to have the EdD and have professors . . . there were some great conversations. [Name of supervisor] brought some great work for us to look at and we had some good discussions. I think we both learned from each other, I think a lot of us came with a very strong sense of social justice, I was much less in tune to those issues, or sensitive and there were some good conversations . . . I learned a lot but I also challenged some of it, because I think there needs to be, it is good not to have everyone coming in with one mind set, it was good to have this black ignorant sheep that is not quite as in tune with it or has not experienced it, because it makes them aware there are people like me out there that really haven't got a background experience in terms of social justice so it made for good dynamics. I was often the lone dissenting voice of things we read. And I still have issues. I still don't think I fully appreciate social justice in schools, I think I have a better appreciation than I had.

Stephen, a superintendant in the United States, agrees that postgraduate research has enabled him to gain deeper insights into the self, his relationship with social justice and that this has influenced his practice. Stephen states:

So the PhD has really helped me in looking at myself and evaluate who I am and my own values and actions and such, so I think it has been a very important process for that and I have seen it in others too, the whole change as they go through this process and they don't just get rings under their eyes and look very tired, and haggered, they actually change, they do get rings under their eyes, they do look exhausted, but they get a free examination of themselves if they are paying attention.

Helen, a member of the Senior Leadership Team in a primary school in England, agrees that doing postgraduate research for her EdD has enabled her to gain important insights into the self, which enables her to reflect on her pedagogical relationships in her teaching. Helen states that her postgraduate research has made her:

more aware of what I'm doing. I'm more aware of my own teaching styles and I'm more aware of the importance of teaching styles, whether they're allowing people to move on and develop or whether they are controlling.

The evidence reveals that postgraduate research provides opportunities for educational leaders to critically reflect on ways in which they are or have been prejudiced and to do the 'I work' necessary to have a better appreciation of social justice in schools. Such reflexivity is evidence informed leadership and has caused what Delamont and Atkinson (2004) call a transformation of identity.

Martin, a programme provider of an EdD postgraduate research programme in the United States with the pseudonym Mississippi River University, agrees that the programme aims in the direction of being emancipatory in terms of the educational leaders gaining self-knowledge but states:

> I think it only becomes really emancipatory when people use the insights that they are gaining through the programmes to try to make real changes in the schools and in themselves. That is really where it becomes liberatory or emancipatory, when you take the task on to change yourself, because it is a daily thing. I say to students all that time that I have been engaged, consciously engaged in anti-racism struggle for forty-five years, and I'm still a racist . . . We don't know what we don't know, and the dominant ideology works through us regardless of how critically conscious we are, and all we can do is to be open to discovering the new ways that we have been racist and sexist and so on. So I think these things only become liberatory when people open themselves up to that and say they are going to devote their life to making changes in themselves and in the system because it's really a way of life liberatory, eman- cipatory work isn't a project or a thing that you do, it is a way of being in the world and a way of life . . . So it's a different notion of leadership that is like our EdD programme, it is collaborative leadership it is about the struggle. It is about working with others to make changes, it is not about being in charge or on top or any of that. It is not having all the answers, it is barely having a glimpse at what the questions are, and then being willing to engage in the hard work of trying to discover something about them.

Michelle, another EdD postgraduate research programme provider from the United States, also agreed that it is important for educational leaders to get to know the self. Michelle states:

> I just did a big study with some colleagues about what educators think about social justice and how they conceive it, and how it plays out in their practices. So many of them thought about social justice in terms of helping all kids pass the standardized tests. So we began to say to them well if you were in a more homogeneous upper-middle class all white school what would social justice look like to you? And the response was so amazing they just were baffled because they didn't know, and then they sort of said well, and repeatedly this

isn't just one person but I got the same response over and over, repeatedly they said things like well I guess those kids would have different kinds of problems. So they were equating social justice with addressing kids' problems but in terms of learning and not thinking about helping kids who are privileged to understand their privileged position or how the global market place works or how keeping prices down and importing goods from China affects the quality of life in other countries to the point where one student last summer when she started reading some things that I asked her to read, said well do we have to talk about this kind of stuff, kids won't enjoy shopping anymore. This is a pretty outrageous statement.

Arthur, an English professional researcher into the EdD postgraduate research programme, affirms that doing postgraduate research on the EdD gives learners the opportunity of becoming more critical. Arthur articulates pedagogical aims for education which tie in closely with those the learners have been unpacking during their intellectual work on the EdD. Arthur states:

I think education actually is about delving more deeply into how you develop knowledge, what that knowledge is and so forth and adopting obviously critical views, critical in the sense of . . . being critical of common sense assumptions about reality, about knowledge and so forth.

Victor, a Russian researcher, pedagogue, policy maker and city officer, also affirms the importance of postgraduate research to help educational leaders learn about themselves, and the systems they live within. However, Victor recognizes that there needs to be conditions for readiness for 'getting to know the self'. Victor acknowledges that Russia has not always been critical within a totalitarian society. However, Victor also recognizes, as does Shields (2007), that so-called democratic societies have lacked a commitment to a critical approach, which is evidenced by minoritized and marginalized communities. Victor and Shields (2007) both appear to be arguing for educational leaders to get to know the self so that they can work for their educational communities. Victor states:

If you live in the society, like totalitarian society which doesn't allow you to criticize, your critical thinking will not develop okay? In deep Soviet times you will say to a child: 'communist party is good, and all others are bad'. Where is the gap to improve your critical thinking? No. If you are living in the society where the democracy is quite high way, it is civilized, I mean critical thinking is much deeper there. That is the key point . . . we are people of post-Soviet society even having this, you know this history 'so-called democracy', I underline it twice, 'so-called democracy', are you with me? Britain and Europe or United States have got the history, the ages of people being able to express their views openly to have the discussions, to have the dialogues and so forth . . . You can't go from a totalitarian country, also totalitarians had quite a long stagnational period, I mean Breshnev's time, and then suddenly . . . it was declared from somewhere, from the TV, 'oh we are free', but to be free has to be learned, to be taught how to be free . . . culture is a layer, and another layer, and another layer, and another layer, and of course in global society, the processes are faster, automatically faster than it used to be when we had very strict borders and so on and so forth. But still, the processes are at different stages, different stages, and we have to go faster in the direction of the child centred pedagogy, definitely, so of course I underline it again, there are very good and very important things which can be called the Russian, or model Russian school's achievements. But having achievements doesn't mean that you are the best, having achievements doesn't mean that you are perfect. There is always a zone of proximal development and so forth for the school as well. For our schools the zone of proximal development is actually the human practice, the curriculum has overwhelmed our teachers sometimes . . . From my postgraduate research, it is easier, when I say easier I mean it is more effective, the conversation itself and the decision making will be easier for me. I will be able to prove to a person that what I am saying is right and it will work. The administration work involves lots of consultancy, it's not consultancy as consultants in an agency. When I visit schools I talk to groups, we talk about making schools better okay. We oral about making the quality of education higher, well this is quite a crude understanding of higher or lower, I mean changing for better. We oral about making schools more effective. We oral about changing and developing teaching practices and so forth. So if I talk to the school head about the particular state of things I may come as the state officer doing some control or whatever it is within my responsibility. But in lots and lots of cases I come and we have a conversation.

Michelle, a postgraduate research EdD programme provider from the United States, also argues that educational leaders need to be critical and reflective practitioners and, like Victor argues, that a child-centred pedagogy is important. Michelle states:

> [T]he purpose of the EdD is to create thoughtful and committed educational leaders who in part of course enhance their own leadership abilities. I always hope that it is also to create leaders to implement policy to change towards equity and social justice. So it is helping them to understand research, understand inequities, just giving them a chance to become really critical and reflective practitioners . . . I think it is critically important, especially again in this era of accountability, where they need to understand what the test scores mean what they don't mean, and what is worth fighting for and what is worth resisting. I think they need to understand all those kinds of things. In the US . . . No Child Left Behind . . . even though it had some really good intentions . . . I don't think there was anything insidious in its intent, has had a lot of unanticipated and unintended consequences that have been pretty negative, because of the heavy emphasis only on the standardized tests, and it has tended to narrow the curriculum and create what the American practitioners often call bubble kids. I don't know if that is a term you know or not, but they do some pre-testing they take a look at the kids who are closest to passing the tests who are on the cusp or on the bubble and then they prescribe additional noon hour lessons, after-school tutoring, Saturday classes or sometimes they take them out of electives and put them into test prep classes so that the school will perform better on the standardized tests. Canada does not have any kind of national mandate for standardized testing and so there are a lot of really significant differences because of that, I think.

However, engaging with getting to know the self, and reconceptualizing practice in light of this new knowledge can be uncomfortable. William, a programme provider and former dean of a university in England, states that the educational leaders:

would ask why do I need all these lenses and why do I need to think in all these kinds of ways? I've got on perfectly well without it in the past. But those that persevere, and the great majority do, get a thrill when they begin to understand what is involved. This happens gradually, but as a teacher you know you've cracked it when people start using such ideas as a matter of course. So if you listen to the character of the discourse and the type of conversation that takes place in the later modules as compared with the earlier modules, you will find that people just talk as a matter or course about such issues. They do so not in a self-conscious or precious way or nervous way, it's become part of their language. They can speak it. They can understand it. I do think it needs to be in the grammar of your thinking if you're to be able then to relate this to your practice and to be able to say, well this is how I understood my practice before, now I know there's another way of looking at it and that way may affect what I do. So . . . all we have by way of evidence is ultimately what people say they do, although we do also see in the conversations that take place around the table for the EdD in particular that such ideas have entered part of their taken-for-granted, their grammar of thinking and it's lovely when that happens. What's lovely too is that a number of people have told me afterwards I thought it was all just fanciful and a waste of my time at the beginning, and why are you bothering me with all these silly abstract ideas, but now I realize I can't cope without them.

The evidence reveals that it is important for educational leaders to make a commitment to critically reflect on ways in which they are prejudiced. This is particularly important if they do not realize they are prejudiced. It is troubling that Michelle's research reveals that professional educationalists believe social justice to be 'helping the poorer kids' in areas where community members have low socio-economic status. A critical and reflective disposition resonates with Stein's (2004) argument presented in Chapter 2 that the educational leaders who have engaged with postgraduate research, and the programme providers of postgraduate research articulate that they are able to get to know themselves better which enables them to recognize social injustice. This connects with Cribb and Gewirtz – cultural justice which focuses on recognition of cultures (Bourdieu, 2000) and respect and tolerance for others (Malmquist, 2009; Cribb and Gewirtz, 2003). This synthesizes with the literature presented in Chapter 2 and appears to be where Every Child Matters and No Child Left Behind are at now: seeking to work for change (Gunter, 2005, p. 70) so that all cultures living together respect one another and recognize one another. Moreover, it is where 'Russian Education – 2020: a model of education for an economy based on knowledge' (2008) is at (Taysum, Pogosian, and Iqbal, 2009). However, such a politics of recognition of many cultures requires individuals from those cultures to be part of a democratic process. The kind of democratic process needs to be redefined (Shields, 2007) as I identified earlier. Using democracy as a mask to ensure that the dominant groups get what they want through 'democratic processes' is not the kind of democracy that is required for citizens to engage meaningfully in worthwhile civic work within a politics of recognition. These leaders identify that evidence informed leadership has enabled them to begin to recognize, gain access to, and then possess the necessary codes, networks of classification and shared meanings of minority and marginalized communities as discussed in Chapter 2. This is an important first step that enables the educational leader to work on behalf of those least advantaged in society and educational systems without pathologizing or essentializing them. The educational leaders who engage with this kind of intellectual work may find accessing such codes uncomfortable because they may realize they have unwittingly been part of the misrecognition of minority and marginalized communities. The empirical evidence also reveals that this kind of commitment to knowing the self and how the self is prejudiced is a lifelong commitment and is a way of life. Such a commitment to a way of living that has been initiated by postgraduate research moves beyond Continuing Professional Development to a more holistic development of the self. Such holistic development engages with being 'good enough' and may move an individual nearer to Maslow's notion of 'self-actualizing'. Leaders who are moving closer to self-actualizing are potentially very good role models for communities. Moreover, such commitments may lead to new understandings of the definition of 'so-called democracy'. The ultimate goal here is to work to enable marginalized and minoritized groups to associate with the educational policies and structures that shape what they can and can not know and do in their communities. Such approaches to working for social justice potentially foster civic engagement where one end of the continuum may be having the chance to vote (Shields, 2007) with one hundred per cent voter turnout, and the other a member of 'a marginalized group' being a successfully elected candidate within a just voting process. This chapter now explores how the leaders used these new ways of thinking and doing to recognize their own prejudices to work for social justice within their communities. This is made possible by moving communities towards a situation where all community members are recognized and respected.

Using a politics of recognition to work for social justice

The educational leaders that I interviewed agreed that they used a politics of recognition to work for social justice though each leader had their own way of interpreting what that meant to them (see Taysum, 2006; Taysum and Gunter, 2008). I now provide some examples of a politics of recognition being included in leaders' practice to work for social justice in their communities. Richard, an educational leader in the district in the United States explained that after doing an EdD postgraduate research programme he was able to use a politics of recognition to work for social justice. He argues he could do this by committing resources to developing continuing professional development programmes that enabled teachers to explore the self in terms of their prejudices that had been hidden from them. Richard states:

> In terms of my leadership it [the EdD postgraduate research programme] definitely made me more sensitive especially because I was controlling millions of dollars of grant funds . . . Before the programme I probably would have emphasized teachers' support of professional development blah blah blah with the grant funds. After the programme I was asking more questions about what is this really doing in terms of the students, in terms of closing the achievement gap, the historic gap we have here. How is this impacting, how are we changing our teaching that is impacting students' learning? Whereas before I was less sensitive to the student needs in terms of minority student needs. I thought . . . I taught it they should have learned it . . . and I was not thinking of a lot of the issues our students have in terms of access and equity

of education that kids have. I think it [the postgraduate research programme] made me more sensitive to those issues than I would have been otherwise as a leader. The other part of it too is that we had a new [leader] come in who is Afro-American who really has equity as a central focus, so it was an aligning of the EdD programme and my new boss being very passionate about social injustices and educational equity. There is a good convergence there between those two forces that helps me to be a lot more aware and sensitive. Initially I was conflicting with them, you know, because initially I was much more into the teachers' professional development and I was more worried about professional development being more traditional and less around having teachers really look at their prejudices and things. So I started to shift from the professional development that we were doing from being traditional to having teachers looking at their prejudices and their biases in their teaching and how that is going to impact on their students who have traditionally not been very successful in our schools. Part of it too is the pattern has been there so long here in the district it was accepted so it was good to have people challenge that; that is just how it has always been how am I going to change that? For thirty years here in the district we have had this achievement gap, we have poured millions of dollars in and we have shown no significant [improvement]. The district has had millions and millions of dollars of grants for closing the achievement gap over the last ten, fifteen, twenty years – and we have shown almost no results. There has been no accountability for getting results. People have actually put in, have tried and put effort in, but no one has made it. So you get these grants and leading these grants to close the achievement gap you think, well they have never done it before. How much accountability can there be in the application that you are actually going to be able to do this? We have made some progress in a few schools, but the EdD programme definitely made me more sensitive to the issues and more aware that it is something that is systemic and you really need systemic leadership looking at the impact of that. You can't just put on a workshop once a year; we did our equity workshop, or whatever we did.

This is affirmed by Jane, an educational leader from the United States. Jane's doctoral dissertation engaged with a professional development programme for teachers that she led. In an interview, Jane helped me to understand how the programme worked by sharing one example, or case with me. Jane begins by giving some background to a teacher she was working with and then goes on to explain how the programme worked using that teacher as an example. Jane states that the teacher:

> was a new teacher and definitely working within a predominantly Hispanic community for the first time. She had worked in a predominantly – probably white – community. I observed that part of the process of the work is that, yes, I am in the classroom modelling the strategies and different curriculum that is culturally relevant to the students, for example this piece of literature introducing that book and providing lessons for her to continue that work with the students. Part two of the work is to go in and observe the teachers and coach them and then have that reflective conversation with them, so it is not just me teaching but me being invited to go in to the classroom when they feel comfortable for me to observe and coach them. She definitely invited me in and I could definitely see the shift, the progress that she made as a critical educator. So on that continuum she really moved, and she moved because of an open heart and open mind. That happens and that is the one thing I think about this work with teachers because it is not top down and mandatory, teachers come to the programme as volunteers they are not being told by their administrator you need to go. So that is part of the process, I do get teachers who are willing to make that shift. They do not all do it.
>
> Like-minded colleagues are not always going to agree on every single issue that emerges, and that is definitely one of the ground rules that we set from the beginning: to agree to disagree, to feel that what is said stays in that safe space so we are not going to leave that space and start gossiping among each other. It is more about how do we support each other. This last year it was really clear politically because we were in an election year, even politically Democrat versus Republican, in that safe space, or independent. It was really interesting that those kinds of issues emerged. What candidate is running for president doesn't emerge but I think that our country elected an African American for president for the first time, it was a pretty amazing year. So a lot of those issues emerged even politically in that safe space and where I am teaching in

a classroom of a teacher who is definitely republican, definitely conservative and definitely not on the same page as I am, politically speaking. I have to say that sometimes, for me, it is a scary position to go into these classrooms and teachers volunteer to be in my programme and I will never turn anyone away who works with predominantly migrant students, but sometimes it is a really difficult job, for me. It always ends up working, Alison, I don't know how to explain it, through relationship and trust but definitely the ideologies politically are not always in sync. We come to the table with different opinions with different experiences of education and different backgrounds and you will find those differences and it is important to put that out there. I have had teachers say, 'Wow I really like the lesson, I love how you put the students in collaborative groups, but I am just not going to do that, I want my students in rows and I don't want them talking to each other.' I have to respect that but the next time I go in and model a lesson, I am going to put the kids back in groups and I am going to continue to model those kinds of strategies and, eventually, maybe teachers will start to shift. That is the hope.

It has direct impact in fact those kinds of strategies, the same strategies that I modelled and that I used with teachers in our safe space in our collaborative meetings are the same strategies that I use with students and often the same materials and curriculum that we use. I had the opportunity to interview, I think, almost fifty students. I can't even remember, but it was quite a large group of students. Half of the students I interviewed in their first language in Spanish, and they definitely could name the strategies. They could talk about the curriculum. They could talk about the kinds of learning that they were doing that was very different to the learning they had done prior to when the teachers weren't using the strategies. They could really compare and contrast and I think that students made it really clear that they felt respected; for the most part, they felt their language was respected, they felt they had choice about the kinds of learning that they could do. The students felt empowered and I think that they felt empowered through a lot of the strategies and, as I said, a lot of the curriculum that was being used.

I would say one of the strands that could be stronger is even the connection with parents and families. I have had the opportunity when I am doing a certain strategy say, for example, reciprocal teaching which is a collaborative reading strategy that students can use without a teacher so they take turns becoming the teacher to question, clarify, summarize and predict their reading. It is a really phenomenal strategy and I have been asked to go to the middle schools in the evenings and offer a session or workshop for parents. For the most part, these sessions are in Spanish and I invite the students to come in and work with the parents so that they can co-teach and co-instruct the strategy with parents and when I have the seminar with teachers I invite a group of students to be the teachers for the teachers, if you know what I mean. When I am teaching reciprocal teaching I don't do the teaching – the students do. The middle school students come in and demonstrate the strategy with each other but the teachers surround them in a circle and just observe and watch the students so it is a very reciprocal learning, it really shifts the power even from me to the students and the students become the teachers of the teachers and the parents so it is a real shift of power.

When I was asked by an administrator to teach reciprocal teaching to his staff. I said well you know what, you have a group, you have all kinds of classrooms of students who have learnt this strategy and let's have them become the teachers. So teachers like [name] and other teachers that I worked with at the site, we were there to support the students because they were in fact their students. So both [name], the Spanish teacher, and [name], an English teacher, we were all working together, oh and another teacher [name], we were there in the classroom as the students were demonstrating the strategy both in English and Spanish in front of a group of teachers at the site. It is a phenomenal way of teaching . . . where students are actually demonstrating, and then there is that wonderful 'question-answer' that happens where the teachers get to ask the students questions, and the students are just brilliant. Then I always offer the students an opportunity to ask their observing teachers any questions that they might have, and that is really amazing what students come up with.

I think that whenever you deepen your pedagogy and your knowledge in education I think it will definitely influence all members of the community, the education community even your administrators your co-workers, the teachers that you directly work with and collaborate with, the families directly and definitely the students, so it is definitely all this knowledge. Really it is drawing on the knowledge of our community too. We are not the experts we are part of that education community. Our students have a lot to teach us as well as our colleagues and our parents. I think that is the process . . . but I have a hard time calling myself a leader or an expert. I want [all] to be treated as professionals and experts even though some of them might be first year, second year, third year in expertise in whatever area we have . . . That came up in my dissertation where teachers didn't feel like I was coming in as an expert, all knowledgeable Wizard of Oz. That is where the relationship was so important so that the teachers could feel that I was there to support them in an authentic way, I wasn't there to judge, that I wasn't there to evaluate them. I was there to support them and if that meant taking their most difficult class and working that through with them, or co-creating curriculum, or just being a listening ear when they needed to cry, I think those things have really built authentic relationships with my colleagues.

Matthew, a headteacher of a primary school in England, which is for children who are four to five years of age in the Foundation Stage and 5 years to 11 years of age from Year 1 to Year 6 which is similar to Kindergarten to Year 6 in The US, agrees with Jane about the importance of building relationships and trust in communities. Matthew states that his postgraduate research programme on the EdD enabled him to use a politics of recognition to work for social justice. He explains that he wanted to build relationships so that all community members could associate with, and contribute to the school's vision. Matthew states:

I think what you want to try and do is to enroll people . . . which means you'd need to do a lot of preliminary work to show people what it's about and I think it's important that people don't feel that it's an imposition that things are being done to them. I mean sometimes you do have to impose certain things . . . But I think that should be used very selectively . . . not just the teachers but with the teaching assistants and anybody else who works in the school. There would be a dinner lady there, a caretaker, etc., and parents for that matter. They get people to enrol into the vision of the school, so that they see what's in it for them but they also see their place in the bigger scheme of things and see that they have a value and that it is important that everyone is pulling in the same direction. But within the context of being able to make mistakes, not being afraid to try things out and not being afraid to use initiative and for that to be also encouraged . . . to make an active contribution to the school, rather than being just passive receivers . . . So again that's a tricky balance and that's why . . . some of the head teachers' standards and the National College of School Leadership bothers me a little bit because for me it's a bit mechanistic and it's as though you can tick your box . . . and then you've got it. But I think it's more complex than that, the relationship is more complex to deal with . . . I think it's art as well as a science, basically.

I explored Matthew's development of the community in a paper with Professor Helen Gunter. I am going to present a key quotation from that paper to reveal how Matthew included children and parents in the work of the school to facilitate all stakeholders to associate with the national curriculum. Taysum and Gunter (2008, p. 195) present the quotation:

We've reached a sort of attainment ceiling with the children. So we have had to have a radical look at the curriculum and all the school systems really, so that we can break through this attainment ceiling. I mean it's trying to get back to certain values in terms of getting the children to have an emotional stake in their learning, and to have the parents to have a similar emotional stake in their children's learning and looking at ways that can happen. So if you go to the QCA curriculum guidelines, then again you're doing a curriculum by numbers and often the content is coming before the school and the content may not relate to the children's own experiences . . . To enable more people to buy into the vision of the school you need to, I believe, open things up, blur the boundaries which can be a curse to some people. It means embracing the community rather than seeing it as a problem and seeing it as an area of potential so altering a mindset (p. 194).

Charles is a principal of a further education college in the United States and has also used a politics of recognition to work for social justice in his community. In particular, he has carefully chosen the area of education he works in to maximize the way he can recognize members of his community who have previously been misrecognized culturally and economically. Charles states:

I have a critical theorist approach to analysing what happened in democracy and social organizations and communities that I serve and my delight as an adult educator is that, and that is why, one of the reasons I am so upset about what has happened in adult education and opposed to Community College and all these other services . . . What we do in adult education at its base is address issues, and imbalances of power and give access to those who have been denied access whether by economics, education, physical or mental ability, age, so adult education by its nature is directed to address the transformation of not having access to having access not having skills to having skills, not having power to having power. That is the educational outcome of what we do at its best and obviously that is an idealist way of looking at it, and I am very comfortable being in this situation, doing this thing, being able to describe it in ways to the community and policy makers above and around me in ways that indicate we are doing something important and I can talk about it in ways that do not sound threatening, that sound, or garner, more appreciation for what we do . . . so education is transformative and adult education is especially transformative and now I can point to, I was always an adult educator in adult education period, but now [as a result of the EdD postgraduate research programme] I understand it on a deeper level, so . . . I was a director of adult education in [name of place] and [name of supervisor] was my advisor who is a brilliant man and I share a lot of values with him and he is one of those who I said it was a privilege to be able to go and talk to him and he knows what he is talking about and he knows what he does not know which is a gift, [laughter] especially for academics. I was working at [name of place] as a director of adult education and he had a project going there as well working with parents in that community but I had worked in adult education at a certain level that is when the Board really valued my administrative skills and began to think about me as being superintendant before the EdD programme.

These educational leaders have argued that their postgraduate research has helped them to use a politics of recognition to work for social justice within their communities (Bourdieu, 2000). Richard and Jane have valued dialogue as a form of communication to begin to understand the extent to which people are able to recognize the practice and thinking of others, particularly those of minority or marginalized communities. This ties in closely with Leal and Saran's (2004) argument that taking time to listen deeply during dialogues to try to reach understandings of all group members' perspectives is important. To be able to recognize minority and marginalized community groups the educational leaders in this research have identified it is important to engage with dialogue to begin to gain a deeper understanding of the different groups that make up a community. I now provide some individual examples of ways dialogue has been used within a community that engages with a politics of recognition. For more examples, I invite the reader to read Taysum (2006) and Taysum and Gunter (2008).

The importance of dialogue for engaging communities in civic work

The evidence reveals that leaders have used dialogue to enable community members to contribute to discourses. A school business manager, who is doing a Masters in Educational Leadership for School Business Management in England, states that her action research enabled a whole school to come together to talk about and work on behaviour management, and states:

> The research investigation I have undertaken has been successful in highlighting the position that the school was in and after a successful intervention establishing where it finds itself now and the potential for further improvement. It has raised the profile of behaviour management within the school and provided the scope for further improvements to enhance the teaching and learning of pupils within the school. (Farrier, 2009).

However, Charles, a principal at an adult education college, articulates that community dialogues need to be conducted while being mindful that they may be conducted in a forum where dominant discourses are still privileged and minoritized voices may not be heard (Shields, 2007) Charles states:

> Last night there was a state endowment which is selecting certain communities in [name of state] to perhaps contribute a lot of money to build healthy

communities broadly defined. [Name of place] here is a very poor immigrant community in [name of place] like gangs and deaths every day and gang shooting and lots of crime and lots of health issues. There is a planning grant for this larger grant and I was at this community planning meeting in [name of place] social agencies some schools there, and it was a community meeting and so community residents were there, and the community agencies . . . but during the course of the evening and seeing the community, there were these other people – not always white, educated, privileged – talking, sucking the air out of the room, and preventing . . . I was just doing discourse analysis . . . to see who was restating what some people were saying, and preventing real other things from being said . . . They don't know what they are doing, but I do [ironic laughter] . . . I guess that is what I am trying to say, real is kids without health care, real is an adult who can not read, and what that means for that adult's life, and real is making that adult read so that adult thinks about herself and her world in a completely different way. So questioning what is real is interesting, but what is more important to me is that woman being able to read. So the people in the halls of [international conference name] who want to impact policy, it is important but it is there, it is just that is where those ideas are and I understand that the policies are supposed to eventually have an impact on the woman who can not read, but it is very complicated. There is more that is happening, and I am here, and I am glad, I am privileged to be here, and I am very happy to be here . . . but that was something in the real world, in my world that, in my working world that I understood, at a much clearer, and deeper level than I would have, had I not gone through the doctorate programme. My research was participatory action research because it built on Habermas and Freire and I see what is not happening here, I see how this is not structured, I see who is dominating and who is bringing the outside culture in to privilege themselves to the detriment of the people you are trying to listen to, and I never would have, I would have intuitively known something was wrong but I would not have been able at such a depth figure out if this person says this they are using a certain diction that makes this person not want to speak, and I would not have the expertise to figure it out. Now the next step to figuring it out is what I should do as a professional, figure out how to create space where this does not happen which is part of this project, maybe this is back to the community taking pieces of information back to the closed system and not having an impact on the community, that is the part that needs to happen. So yes, you can understand it, so what? So what can be different for those people? How can you create something that makes a difference in their lives? So how I work can make a difference to hundreds of thousands of people who live here in [name of place] so rising to the level simply of policy is important but not immediate for what I want to do with the knowledge I have.

Therefore, it is important that when engaging with community dialogue there are general principles and guidelines available that can be consulted when interpreting educational policy such as No Child Left Behind and Every Child Matters. These need to be engaged with in educational settings in a joined-up way that, as Charles indicates, will include those that work in health, crime and justice, social welfare, policy makers, government departments and associated professional bodies. The need for such principles and guidelines for educational leaders to frame dialogues agrees with Pring (2000), who suggests professional ethics are a search for rules for right thought and right behaviour. This is more than just doing the right thing, it is also having the right kind of thinking. In other words, ethics is a search for rules to understand what is moral and what is immoral. Trying to work this out is very difficult and calls for universal ethical principles that can be applied in all situations. Such universal principles have three different properties at their centre. The first is consequences, the second is rights and the third is virtues. These elements are included in Jones and McNamee's useful adaptation of Kohlberg's levels of moral development presented in Chapter 6. The levels may be used to assess the stage and quality of the ethical framework of the dialogue so that it is inclusive and democratic in the sense that it is socially just (Cribb and Gewirtz, 2003). There may be conditions of readiness for the dialogue before it can move to the next stage of the framework with the aim of all community members moving from punishment and obedience to when the morality of the given convention or society is adopted Jones and McNamee (2000, p. 133). This may then move to the third stage where community members conform to their perception of the social norm. When this has been achieved the fourth stage may be engaged where the rules and norms of society are respected and give rise to certain duties, in this book such enterprise is called civic work. The next stage is right thought and action that is determined by norms and rules. However, community members are actively involved in their construction (ibid.). This is Cribb and Gewirtz's (2003) association with a 'social contract'. The final, and sixth, stage is where community members are guided by a concern for universal ethical principles that guides all action. In Chapter 6 the arguments were presented that there are tensions between who is actively associating with their educational communities and who is marginalized. The notion of democracy needs to be redefined in terms of inclusion. Martin, a postgraduate research programme provider and professor at a United States university with the pseudonym Mississippi River University, says he has worked on an equity project that tries to recognize the need to redefine what is meant by democracy and inclusion. Martin states:

> I think that there are ways to construct school-wide learning environments where teachers are collaboratively engaged in doing research and assessment . . . What we found was that the teachers were very anxious to engage in evaluative research and action research that was directly geared into their instructional practices, but they didn't really know how to do it. So when we provided the training for them to do that, and provided basically space, for them to work together on that, they embraced that. Another model that all of the schools in the [name of network] embraced enthusiastically, including the principals, was the lesson study model from Japan, where they designed a lesson collaboratively based on research and then one of them would teach the lesson and the others would observe and then they would design a new lesson based on what they learned from that, so they started to build a culture within the school of research-based practices and doing their own research on their own practices. What we found was that teachers in all these low income schools that were all in programme improvement and all being heavily criticized by the government because of their test scores . . . We found that teachers enthusiastically embraced these opportunities when they were provided to them in a structured and meaningful way . . . what we said there was standardized testing is the coin of the realm right. So we did see improvements in test scores, it didn't mean that the schools were always able to hit the benchmarks that the government laid out for them. It didn't mean that the schools didn't

continue to have 50 per cent turnover rates in the student body, that kind of thing. But I guess what we found is you are able to teach to the standards that are supposedly the basis of the tests but you can do that in creative ways, you can do that in the ways that honour the background language, culture of the students or not. So we try to work with teachers based on the reality of the pressures that they faced in their schools and in their districts, and try to develop support programmes for the kids so that they were getting the basic skills necessary to do okay on these tests. Even if No Child Left Behind were to disappear, we believe that accountability is important and maybe some kind of standardized tests are an appropriate part of an accountability system. But we just don't believe that they should be the only element of an accountability system and that schools need to be tracking and measuring other kinds of things as well. Whether it is ways of thinking about citizenship, ways of thinking about what the teachers are doing for students beyond preparing them for tests. The degree to which teachers are and schools are involving parents in real ways. There are a lot of things that we can look at and begin to measure and assess and take account of that would provide a more, a fuller picture of accountability of schools to their communities. So No Child Left Behind and all that, the real evil is not the accountability. The evil is using inappropriate tests in inappropriate ways, so.

Here, the role of dialogue is an important way of enabling community members to contribute to the interpretation of policies and structures that shape their lives. Such dialogues would need to take place in a step-by-step way, moving through Jones and McNamee's (2000) six stages. However, what is key to progression through these stages is a cooperative and trusting context where communities have the chance to reach provisional consensus before moving on to the next step. Such a method enables participants to examine their own values systems in relation to the topic or issue of the dialogue. Therefore, the participants need to search for truth while reconciling issues of power among different cultures. Understanding, respect and tolerance are important and need to be located within an ethical framework so that the notion of evidence informed leadership in education is considered in terms of facilitating building trust. Therefore, communities need opportunities for dialogue where they can be critical and reflective in the way they engage with the problems of public life. Using Jones and McNamees' adapted framework, the balance between the self and society can be explored in an active way rather than through passive helplessness. This ties in closely with the 'I and the we' of Ubuntu where citizens can think through the kinds of relationships needed for such civic work. Moreover, these issues need to be examined in safe spaces, and may need new and innovative ways of capturing the dialogues. For example, Nancy, an educational leader from the United States who has completed her doctorate, says that communities may be able to associate with discourses through different media, such as digital stories. Nancy states: 'I feel much more useful because making digital stories is something the community can access and can really be moved by'. However, it is important to note that Martin, a postgraduate research programme provider and professor in the United States, states that: 'the digital stories are only a way to focus the community dialogue's comments'. It is important to explore how the dialogues can enable all community members to associate with the development of personal, social, cultural and political processes and relationships.

Conclusions

To sum up, this research has demonstrated how community leaders who have engaged with evidence informed leadership are sowing the seeds for building inclusionary relationships of trust and opportunity for cooperative dialogue for civic work. The leaders have argued that they have been able to engage with a politics of recognition which means they have been able to recognize marginalized and minoritized groups after they began to do some 'I work'. By 'I work', I mean work to know the self better so that prejudices that may lead to misrecognition of others can be critically reflected upon with humility and honesty, enabling authentic recognition to take place. Once the educational leaders are able to recognize the minoritized groups, they are able to facilitate civic work through dialogues so that community members can begin to associate with the educational institutions' visions. The evidence revealed that the dialogues need to be conducted within ethical frameworks that have clear guidelines and principles for all participants. There is a danger that dialogues that do not operate within such frameworks may allow dominant discourses to replicate inequalities which is a barrier to social justice. Thus the evidence has demonstrated how educational institutions and their communities may practice building relationships with each other that may continue to develop, refresh and sustain day by day (Beatty, 2007). In this way, a sharp focus on economic, cultural and associational justice (Cribb and Gewirtz, 2003) may be maintained, and communities may have a window of opportunity to work towards an ecological equilibrium that it is self-sustaining.

References

Beatty, B. (2007), Going through the emotions: leadership that gets to the heart of school renewal. *Australian Journal of Education*, 51 (3), 328–40.

Bourdieu, P. (2000), *Pascalian Meditations*. Cambridge: Polity.

Cribb, A. and Gewirtz, S. (2003), Towards a sociology of just practices; an analysis of plural conceptions of justice. In C. Vincent (ed.), *Social Justice Education and Identity*. London: RoutledgeFalmer.

Delamont, S., and Atkinson, P. (2004), Qualitative research and the postmodern turn. In M. Hardy and A. Bryman (eds), *Handbook of data analysis*. London: Sage.

Farrier, W. (2009), How to move forward to improve behaviour management in a special school. *British Educational Leadership, Management, Administration Society Annual Conference*. Sheffield, July 2009.

Hardy, M. and Bryman A. (eds) (2004), *Handbook of data analysis*. London: Sage.

Jones, C. and McNamee, M. (2000), Sports, ethics and philosophy; context, history, prospects in *Sport, Ethics and Philosophy*, 5 (2), 131–46.

Kuz'minov, I. and Framin, I. (eds) (2008), *Russian Education – 2020: A model of education for an economy based on knowledge* in Russian (RE). Moscow: Publishing house of HSE.

Leal, F. and Saran, R. (2004), A dialogue on the Socratic dialogue, act two. In P. Shipley (ed.), *Occasional Working Papers in Ethics and Critical Philosophy*, 3.

Malmquist, H. (2009), Social diversity and the principle of tolerance: a philosophical analysis. *Society for the Furtherance of Critical Philosophy Annual Conference*. Chichester, July 2009.

Pring, R. (2000), *Philosophy of Educational Research*. London: Continuum.

Saran, R. and Neisser, B. (eds) (2004), *Enquiring Minds*. Stoke-on-Trent: Trentham Books.

Shields, C. (2007), A failed initiative: democracy has spoken – or has it? *Journal of Cases in Educational Leadership*, 10 (1), 14–21.

Stein. S. (2004), *The Culture of Education Policy*. New York: Teachers College Press, Colombia University.

Taysum, A. (2006), The learning journeys of educational leaders. Unpublished doctoral thesis, University of Birmingham.

Taysum, A. and Gunter, H. (2008), A critical approach to researching social justice and school leadership in England. *Education, Citizenship and Social Justice*, 3 (2), 183–99.

Taysum, A., Pogosian, V. and Iqbal, M. (2009), Comparing contemporary educational policies in England, The US, Russia and Pakistan; multi-cultural perspectives within the global village. *European Conference for Educational Research*. Vienna, September (forthcoming).

Chapter 8

Evidence Informed Leadership Takes Time Because It Matters

The final chapter presents a summary where the argument that it is important to move forward with evidence informed leadership in educational settings is presented. This is particularly so, if the English Every Child Matters and the United States No Child Left Behind agendas are to be met. Evidence informed leadership is important because it enables educational leaders, and the communities they serve, to critically analyse and reflect. This may lead to people gaining new ways of thinking and doing which leads to people having greater self-knowledge, which in turn enables them to recognize if they have been colluding in their own exclusion. Such an approach may enable citizens to recognize new career and life trajectories that were not considered possible before. It may also enable citizens to think through how they might associate more with their own community. This might be achieved through developing their understanding and tolerance of others, and taking up shared civic responsibility working within policies that shape economic and cultural structures. Evidence informed leadership may be one way of moving towards removing barriers to social justice. Moreover, there is scope for the academy to support communities in developing evidence informed leadership through, for example, postgraduate research programmes. It is hoped that such an endeavour will bridge the gap between the academy and communities in educational settings.

Mapping the recent history of educational policies it is clear that there has been a shift in the balance of power from control of the curriculum by the teaching profession to control of the curriculum by the government/Congress. This has happened with the right intentions, to give every child an equal opportunity with regard to the No Child Left Behind Title 1 reforms and the Every Child Matters reforms. However, this has led to the professional educationalists not being able to do what they do best, which is get to know their students and provide learning opportunities that are learner-centred. Such culturally relevant learning is arguably more respectful to the learner. Such an approach does not include teaching to a test using a prescribed curriculum that ignores a 'readiness to learn'. However, appropriate formative and summative assessment will still be essential for the learning process to be successful.

The written policy and the realization of that policy where the rubber meets the road, needs to be community-centred and learner-centred. This may be an important step to facilitating the learners becoming motivated because they have more ownership of what they are going to learn and it makes sense to them and their lives. Internal motivation for learning, and potential enjoyment of the learning process, may escalate as they begin to experience success in their learning journeys. This may be coupled with external motivation if they begin to experience examination success. Examination success is preferred to operating in a testing system that labels children and adult learners as failures. Such an attack on the children and adult learners' self-esteem may prevent them from achieving their full potential. This has massive implications for the well-being of the child and adult learners, their families and the community. The next step needs to be engaging communities 'democratically' in the learning process and building pedagogical relationships based on evidence, positive regard and respect and tolerance for people who become citizens fully engaged in civic work. The book explored how this might be achieved in a step-by-step process and focused on possible solutions to the problems each chapter raised. It did this by presenting authentic and systematic ways in which educational leaders and their communities can examine the taken-for-granted assumptions wrapped up in educational policies. The book provided evidence-informed ways in which to confront such 'common sense views' when working for social justice and moving from policy as text to policy as discourse in communities.

Those who lead schools, arguably headteachers and senior leaders, are in receipt of policies that are developed away from the location within which they are to be realized. The policy as text is arguably constructed so there is little room for interpretation other than how the policy writers wanted it to be interpreted (Ball, 2006). Policies are political, and the process of policy formation can be random, or lucky (Ball, 2006). Randomness and luck are not part of a systematic and rigorous approach to policy making that educational communities can learn to systematically and democratically engage with. In short, it might be argued that 'randomness and luck' are not the stuff of ethical civic work. Leaders need to be involved in the writing of policy as text so that they can develop the knowledge, thinking tools and experience required to develop policy that is meaningful to their particular communities. Moreover, leaders may be able to facilitate cultural groups within their communities to share the writing of policy as text and the operationalization of policy as discourse. Such policy work is community-based education. Community-based education (Gandin and Apple, 2002; Furman and Greunewald, 2004) has the potential to give community members more control over how they experience their lives, and how they recognize and celebrate the diversities of their different cultures. The community can choose the themes that they want to explore, and their teachers can take these themes and use them to tune into how to make the acquisition of literacy and numeracy skills more meaningful. Finding different 'ways in' to reach individuals' internal motivation to learn something is important. This kind of pedagogic work can only take place when relationships have been developed and the teacher has begun to recognize what themes may be of interest to different members of the community. Community-based learning may also foster the coupling of economic and cultural justice through facilitating a community's association with the rules and structures that shape their members' identities. Evidence informed leadership of communities who collaborate in the writing, operationalization and leadership of policies as text and discourse may be emancipatory and contribute to the removal of barriers to social justice. Developing self-awareness is important to facilitate evidence informed leadership, and thinking tools may be required to facilitate evidence informed leadership as a way to bridge the gap between the different groups in educational settings. The argument I have presented thus far suggests that economic and cultural injustice may be embedded if educational policies do not recognize economic and cultural differences and do not include democratic associational justice. Thinking tools such as critical analysis, reflection and the ability to be reflexive may help practitioners develop evidence informed leadership. Such tools may help learners to understand the interplay between what shapes what they can and can not do and the power issues involved. This may free them up from structures that are constraining, which is arguably liberating.

The science and art of teaching, or the pedagogy and pedagogical relationships

that are built between the postgraduate research provider and leader are important with the presentation of these kind of thinking tools. This is because the
leaders will also need to build their capacity to be ethical researchers if they are
to verify evidence before evidence-informed decisions are made. The Learning
to CARE framework of critical reflection and reflexivity helps leaders map their
relationship with their postgraduate research. Lunt's (2002) framework is an
excellent thinking tool to help postgraduate research think about different
modes of knowledge. Finally, Gunter's (2005) framework is a powerful thinking tool that helps postgraduate researchers think about their research and
the reflexive relationship with the evidence informed leadership with regard
to whether it is instrumental, evaluative, emancipatory, or to further understanding. Therefore, these thinking tools, when used on a university site, have
the potential to build leadership capability, capacity, and to begin to work for
collective intelligence within democratic communities that care about the self
and for others. The leader doing postgraduate research becomes a public intellectual within the university which acts as a connector of discourses. As such, the
university is a site of public and moral debate that stands against the erosion of
the public space where no political, cultural, cognitive or particular ideology is
dominant. This tool enables those engaging with postgraduate research to consider their research problem and research design from different epistemological
approaches and to be transparent about the way in which they justify what they
have accepted and what they have rejected with this important choice. Thus
fostering critical engagement, reflection and reflexivity for evidence informed
leadership that is realistic and relates to current issues may enable leaders to
work for change in their educational communities which might include enhancing community and civic responsibility. This is particularly important where
leaders from different agencies within Children's Services need to work together
with the learner at the centre.

However, it is important to note that teaching can be defined as both trying
to, and succeeding in, imparting that which is worthwhile and *moral* to the
learner(s). I recommend that further research be carried out to examine quality
in postgraduate research; doctoral and masters programmes' pedagogy. This
would further develop the research base for the claims made here to serve as
powerful maps for policy and practice. Such research would also need to address

how to frame teaching and learning in postgraduate research that is moral. This is particularly important if evidence informed leadership is to play a part in removing the barriers to social justice.

There are tensions between who is actively associating with their educational communities, and who is marginalized. The notion of democracy needs to be redefined in terms of inclusion. This means that there are equality of opportunities to contribute to the decision making processes that shape the 'I and the we'. The role of dialogue was presented as an important way of enabling community members to contribute to the interpretation of policies and structures that shape their lives. Such dialogues would need to be taken step by step in a cooperative and trusting context where communities have the chance to reach provisional consensus before moving on to the next step. Such a method enables participants to examine their own values' systems in relation to the topic or issue of the dialogue. For dialogue to work the participants need to search for the truth while reconciling issues of power among different cultures. Understanding and respecting tolerance is important here while working within ethical frameworks to engage with evidence informed leadership. If dialogue occurs under these conditions there is an opportunity to gain understanding within the community which is an important step towards finding solutions to society's problems.

The evidence presented in Chapter 7 revealed how community leaders who have engaged with evidence informed leadership are sowing the seeds for building inclusionary relationships of trust and opportunity for cooperative dialogue for civic work. The leaders have argued that they have been able to engage with a politics of recognition which means they have been able to recognize marginalized and minoritized groups after they began to do some 'I work'. By 'I work', I mean work to know the self better so that prejudices that may lead to misrecognition of others can be critically reflected upon with humility, honesty, and then eliminated. Once the educational leaders are able to recognize the minoritized groups, they are able to facilitate civic work through dialogues so that community members can begin to associate with the educational institutions' visions. The evidence revealed that the dialogues need to be conducted within ethical frameworks that have clear guidelines and principles for all participants. There is a danger that dialogues that do not operate within such frameworks may allow dominant discourses to replicate inequalities which is a barrier to social justice. Thus the evidence has demonstrated how educational institutions and their communities may practice building relationships with each other that may continue to develop, refresh and sustain day by day (Beatty, 2007). In this way, a sharp focus on economic and cultural justice may be maintained and communities may have a window of opportunity to work for an ecological equilibrium that it is self-sustaining.

As a final note to this book, I believe I have experienced a shift in identity on my learning journey on the EdD and in the privileged position of being a programme provider and leader of masters and doctoral programmes for educational leaders in a leading university. I would be inclined to position myself as moving between stage 3 and stage 4 of the Learning to CARE framework. I believe this learning journey to be one of the most valuable periods of my life. This knowledge has enabled me to begin to understand how I am positioned within the field of educational leadership. Critically reflecting and becoming increasingly reflexive in my practice has enabled me to see how I have played my part in colluding in my own exclusion. Some of the most important discoveries I have made connect this with issues of social justice. I have learned much from the thinking tools that are presented in this book. I have also learned more about the research process and how it is difficult to hear marginalized voices for many reasons. Yet it is the dominant discourses that perhaps have the most to gain from listening to these marginalized voices. I remain committed to trying to understand the complexities of respondents' representations of their realities. I have learned that I have much to learn about the interplay between structures such as educational policy and agency, such as what educational leaders choose to do and choose not to do, and how this connects with issues of power. In trying to 'problematize' the common sense view, I recognize that my learning journey on the EdD has been very uncomfortable at times. I have had my constructs challenged and challenged again and perhaps this kind of construing and re-construing is not for the faint hearted. However, this journey has also been incredibly exciting. Perhaps I am becoming more comfortable with being uncomfortable, which is a disposition I am working hard to sustain, in this incredibly beautiful and at times incredibly violent world.

This research has been incredibly exciting and I recognize that my own identity would not have shifted in the way that it has without the support of colleagues from the postgraduate research programmes that I have been a student on, taught on, initiated, generated, developed, and led, and from those who gave up their valuable time to help me in this research. I believe that it will shape the rest of my career as a researcher and professional educationalist. As such, postgraduate research has enabled me to develop as a career researcher and engage with evidence informed leadership. Perhaps there is scope to further research the extent to which doctoral study and postgraduate research can develop sustainable educational leadership while building leadership capacity.

I also recognize that this research and my learning journey on the EdD has shaped and will probably continue to shape the rest of my life holistically, in other words every aspect of my life. This has certainly been emancipatory and a learning journey of value. My hopes and aspirations for this research is that it might make a small contribution to making other people's windows of opportunities become reality.

References

Ball, S. J. (2006), *Education Policy and Social Class*. London: Routledge Taylor and Francis Group.

Beatty, B. (2007), Going through the emotions: leadership that gets to the heart of school renewal. *Australian Journal of Education*, 51 (3), 328–40.

Furman, C. and Greunewald, A. (2004), Expanding the landscape of social justice: a critical and ecological analysis. *Education Administration Quarterly*, 40 (1), 47–76.

Lunt, I. (2002), Integrating Academic and Professional Knowledge: Constructing the Practitioner-Researcher. Available at: http://www.qut.edu.au/dresa/CPE/ProfDocs/Papers/Scott_paper.doc (accessed 3 April, 2003).

Gandin, L. and Apple, M. (2002), Challenging neo-liberalism building a democracy: creating the citizen school in Porto Alegre Brazil. *Journal of Education Policy*, 17 (2), 259–79.

Gunter, H. (2005), Conceptualizing Research in Educational Leadership. *Educational Management Administration and Leadership*, 33 (2), 165–80.

Index

academy 1, 4, 6, 8–9, 13, 23, 44, 85, 98, 102, 131, 157
accountability 21–2, 139, 143, 154
achievement gap 142–3
administrators 4, 28, 99, 144, 146
adult education 149–50, 158
AERA (American Educational Research Association) 11, 28, 67, 102
agencies 7, 23, 27, 37, 40, 44–5, 47–9, 53, 91, 105, 138, 160, 162
agendas 6–7, 9, 15, 22, 24, 37, 43, 48, 50, 53, 157
agent 3, 45, 47, 62, 69, 75, 88–9, 91, 118
angst 116, 132–3
Apple, M. 52, 90, 159
application 59, 90, 107, 143
Aristotle 3, 39, 69, 124
aspirations 27, 49, 96
assessment 26, 28–9, 153
assessment for learning (AfL) 26
Atkinson, P. 9, 131, 135
Atkinson, R. C. 26–9
Australia 4
authority 21, 44–5
  moral 124

balance 1, 50, 63, 74, 120, 126–9, 155–6, 162
  of power 14, 19, 31, 157
  in school calendar 16
Ball, S. 14–15, 21, 29–30, 38, 41, 51–2, 79, 90, 109, 158
Barnett, R. 3, 41, 64, 68, 79, 105

barriers 7, 23, 30, 37, 43–6, 48, 52–3, 65, 70, 88–90, 108–9, 111–12, 118–19, 156, 159, 161
Bartlett, S. 19, 21
Beatty, B. 40, 128–9, 162
behaviour
  bad 26, 31, 117
  management 150
  right 121, 123, 152
beliefs 89, 103, 108, 118–19
benefit 15, 127
BERA (British Educational Research Association) 11, 67
Bertaux, D. 25
Bertaux-Wiame, I. 25
Biddle, B. 4, 6, 57
Bourdieu, P. 25, 29, 44–8, 50, 68, 74, 78–9, 88–91, 105–10, 117, 132, 140, 149
Broadhead, P. 23, 28
Brooks, F. 46
Burton, D. 21
Burton, N. 27

capital 44–5, 87–91, 108
  cultural 45–7, 123
  economic 44
  human 25
  social 44
  symbolic 45
career 1–2, 6, 9, 15, 45, 48, 68, 71, 76, 78, 91, 106–7, 157
change
  and agents 47–8, 69
  to current state 3, 16–17

13524169R00102

Printed in Great Britain
by Amazon.co.uk, Ltd.,
Marston Gate.